GHOSTS

of Gettysburg

II

Spirits, Apparitions and Haunted Places of the Battlefield

by
Mark Nesbitt

Second Chance Publications
Gettysburg, PA 17325

Published by Second Chance Publications
P.O. Box 3126
Gettysburg, PA. 17325

ISBN 10: 0-9752836-8-5
ISBN 13: 978-0-9752836-8-4

Photos by the author unless otherwise credited.
Cover design by Ryan C. Stouch

To Dani
A kindred spirit…

In great deeds something abides. On great fields something stays. Forms change and pass; bodies disappear; but spirits linger, to consecrate ground for the vision-place of souls. And reverent men and women from afar, and generations that know us not and that we know not of, heart-drawn to see where and by whom great things were suffered and done for them, shall come to this deathless field, to ponder and dream; and lo! the shadows of a mighty presence shall wrap them in its bosom, and the power of the vision pass into their souls.

—Major General Joshua Chamberlain
Gettysburg, October 3,1889

Table of Contents

Foreword

More than a decade before the Civil War, Nathaniel Hawthorne, in his introduction to the novel *The Scarlet Letter*, observed: "There is a fatality, a feeling so irresistible and inevitable that it has the force of doom, which almost invariably compels human beings to linger around and haunt, ghostlike, the spot where some great and marked event has given the color to their lifetime." While Hawthorne was writing of Salem, Massachusetts, his recognition of the power of the "spirit of place" is no less true of Gettysburg. And if this spirit can compel so many thousands of visitors to Gettysburg annually—a visit many choose to make again and again—is it enough merely to attribute that power to a creative imagination or sense of history? Or is there more?

The author of this book, Mark Nesbitt, believes there is. And as someone who has had the pleasure of knowing him for many years, I can say with certainty that he is not the kind of person given to "all kinds of marvelous beliefs, trances, visions or strange sights." But, as Washington Irving did with the old Dutch villages along the Hudson River in such stories as "The Legend of Sleepy Hollow" and "Rip Van Winkle," Mark has clearly established that Gettysburg is indeed a neighborhood that "abounds with local tales, haunted spots, and twilight superstitions."

Dr. Walter L. Powell
Gettysburg
August 28, 1992

On Interludes With The Other World

I balanced all, brought all to mind,
The years to come seemed waste of breath,
A waste of breath the years behind
In balance with this life, this death.

—William Butler Yeats

Before I moved to Gettysburg twenty years ago, I lived in northern Ohio near Cleveland in a town with a population of over 80,000 people. Having a number of industries in the city, the area was a melting pot of races and nationalities, politics and religions. Surely, with as large a population and with as many pious, God-fearing, and superstitious souls as there were, in twenty years I should have heard some ghost stories.

But I remember only two in twenty years. One was about an orphanage—appropriately named "Gore Orphanage"—which burned to the ground several decades before I or any one of my friends was born. They said on certain crisp autumn nights you could hear the children who died in the fire screaming for help. Needless to say, as soon as any one of us got his driver's license, a nocturnal trip past Gore Orphanage with a carload of pals was obligatory. The charred ruins were indeed visible from the roadway. But, no one that I knew, sad to say, ever heard a thing.

The other story—which can't even be classified as a ghost story—was that ancient hack about the couple out parking after a date. They had heard on the radio of an escaped lunatic from a local asylum. There was a rustle in the bushes. The young man goes out to investigate and tells his girl to lock all the doors and, no matter what happens, not to open them. Five minutes pass. Then ten. After fifteen minutes she begins to hear a quiet tapping and slow scraping on the roof of the car. It continues for an hour and longer. Heeding her boyfriend's command, she curls up, covering her head in fear. The tapping goes on all night until the sun rises, when finally it ceases. Nearly mad with fear, she starts at the sound of a knock at the window. It is the local constable, sent by her frantic parents to find her and her boyfriend. "What ever you do," he says, helping her out of the car to a waiting ambulance, "don't look back." As she sits down in the ambulance, she cannot help herself. She takes a quick look back at the car. There, hanging upside down over the roof of the car, his blood dripping rhythmically and his fingernails barely able to scrape the roof, was her boyfriend who had died only moments before.

Thrilling, but how many communities have had that same lover's lane lunatic prowling about committing mayhem?

Two stories in twenty years.

But when I moved to Gettysburg, in a quarter of that time I'd heard enough stories—augmented by some contemporary research—to collect into *Ghosts of Gettysburg*. In fact, there were more than enough. Hence this second volume, *Ghosts of Gettysburg II*.

When *Ghosts of Gettysburg* first came out I had expected more than a few skeptics to accuse me of either: a) making the stories up; or, b) being completely crazy, along with my sources, for believing in these sightings.

Those are two comments I have yet to hear. Perhaps it is because I usually preface my talks to various groups about the book with a comment about my methodology: I tried to include only the stories which I had heard from at least two different sources who experienced the event at different times or from two different sources who themselves had heard it from different unrelated people at different times.

Another thing I like to say to those skeptical of people who see visions of spirits in the night, is that people are normally not likely to report something that will expose them to ridicule...unless they are so convinced by the undeniability of the experience, that they are compelled to tell about it.

The two types of comments I *did* receive after the book came out were surprising. First, there were people calling me on the phone, writing to me, and coming up to me to tell me about their own paranormal experiences at Gettysburg. I received letters, calls and comments from people in Virginia, Ohio, Pennsylvania, New York, Montana, California—and Gettysburg—who had had strange experiences on the Gettysburg Battlefield. It seems as if the publication of a book chronicling other peoples' interludes with the other world somehow validated their unbelievable experiences on the fields where so much energy dissipated.

The other comment I received was even more astounding: "You know that ghost you wrote about at Devil's Den? Some friends and I saw him and he looks just the way you described him!"

*   *   *

So, just what *is* still going on out there where the fire of youth and patriotic passion was doused thousands and thousands of times over in three short days?

I think some people want me to explain why the apparitions have occurred, and continue to occur, and why seemingly unexplainable and illogical visions pop up out of nowhere and just as suddenly and inexplicably return to wherever it was they came from. I cannot fully explain it. Some people look toward the existence of ghosts as a sort of proof, a validation that there is another life after this one, that death is not the final Victor, but merely the Great Imposter.

I am aware that some sociologists and paranormalists who have studied numerous events have attempted to classify the visions. I suppose it is their desire to study them scientifically. Yet, since the apparitions cannot be repeated under controlled conditions whenever we want to repeat them, they cannot be literally classified as scientific. But collected as they have been in this and the previous book, they can be studied.

It seems though that many people who have never seen an apparition are resolute: To them there are no such things as ghosts. It also seems that those who *have* seen or experienced something paranormal are just as adamant: They may not want to call it a ghost, but they are absolutely certain of what they saw.

Yet whether we've seen some unexplainable vision or not, there is something to those odd feelings we sometimes get. We've all been sitting and have had the feeling that someone behind is looking at us. The "feeling" that we are being stared at is so strong that we are often compelled to look in that direction, and are normally greeted by a face which quickly looks away. Why do we not want to believe it when the feeling is the same and strong enough to make us turn and look and there happens to be no one there?

We also acknowledge that there are certain people who are more sensitive than others to the presence of these as yet unexplainable sightings. Truly, some of us have a little extra perception into that unseen realm. And then there are those people who have never had a paranormal experience in their lives and have come to Gettysburg and experienced one for the first time.

So the feelings extend to certain places as well. Most people, at one time or another have experienced an uncomfortable feeling walking at night in certain areas or in certain buildings. The heart begins to pump faster, the scalp tingles, and the walking pace picks up. Walking through a cemetery (as I often did when I lived in the National Cemetery at Gettysburg) most people will feel uncomfortable. Is it merely the power of suggestion, or is it the place itself?

Most of history has been written in human blood with a bayonet for a quill. We've warred for land, for love, for lord, for riches, for royalty, for rape. We've killed and suffered for peace, for God, for country. Certainly, of all places on this earth, a battlefield would hold for many years the strong emotional remnants—like a lingering scent or a fingerprint in the soft dust of time—of those who fought and died there.

Battlefields where Americans have struggled and were slain are special places because of one singular attitude Americans historically have had. We've always been known for our savvy as tradesmen. Furs, foodstuffs, precious minerals, land, weapons, baseball cards, used cars. We've always liked to think of ourselves as honest in a trade, and shrewd—getting what we want for what we no longer need. Americans always like to think they've traded one thing for something better. The battlefield fouls that all up.

A man's dying is a very precious thing. You'd like to be certain that somehow you've traded life for something more important. But on a battlefield, there are no good bargains. A soldier trades his life for a few feet of terrain, for a little bit of higher ground, or a few yards of seawall or rock fence. No wonder there are disgruntled spirits lingering on American battlefields.

And, as long as Americans continue to fight, there will be those broken, wandering, souls in rebellion, and the cries of the doomed will fade into mere whispers softly echoing on those battlefields from beyond, perhaps forever. Gettysburg is now, and certainly will continue to be, one of those places where the echoes can be heard.

To those who are analytical, several truly scientific theories, when looked at broadly, hint at being able to explain the existence of life after death, even if in another form and in another world.

Three theories have emerged from the science of physics that might apply to answering the question whether there is existence in some form after death. One of the laws of thermodynamics states that the total sum of energy in the universe cannot be added to or reduced, that it remains constant, but merely changes forms.

Ever since Einstein's formula of $E = MC2$ was confirmed, we have realized that matter and energy are indeed interchangeable, and that time—using the speed of light as an absolute—is an inescapable part of the equation as well. Now if matter and energy are the same thing in different forms, and if, according to the laws of thermodynamics, energy is constant, then the only kicker in trying to apply some real physical laws to prove the existence of life after death, is time. Since we are convinced death is irreversible and time cannot be made to go back, it would seem impossible for someone once dead to appear alive again.

Some recent theories are beginning to explain even this. Parallel universes—invisible to one another yet existing side by side and simultaneously—may help us understand how, while changing form, energy can continue to exist irrespective of time constraints. It is a theory that is gaining more followers all the time to help explain some physical anomalies scientists are discovering throughout the universe. Could death be just a door to that other, simultaneously existing universe? Could the laws of our strictly forward-moving time be meaningless there? Could the energy from our own dissolving or dying matter—since energy cannot be destroyed—merely change locations as it changes form? Could the sightings described in this and other books be tiny tears in *this* reality's fabric providing a brief glimpse into the usually invisible, but also very real, parallel-existing world? Could the parallel universe—this world's counterfeit—be the place we've heard described in literature as "heaven" or "paradise," the place of the Great Light from which those individuals who have had near-death experiences return and talk about? And is there a limbo place where perturbed spirits dwell that is in this parallel universe whose door is sometimes thick and sometimes thin, sometimes opaque and sometimes glassine?

Two things we know for sure: We don't know all there is to know about energy and our generation is not at the end of all knowledge. It was only in 1927, after having lived with the most abundant and universal energy source for millions of years that scientists realized that it was nuclear fusion that energized our own sun. Suddenly, after all those millennia, we understood.

Perhaps that is how it will be one day with ghosts and life after death and currently unexplained energies. Perhaps we will understand enough about energy and time and parallel universes to, if not control our journey into the other world, at least know how it happens. Until then, all we can do is ponder...

A Wrinkle In Time

I have eaten your bread and salt.
I have drunk your water and wine.
The deaths ye died I have watched beside,
And the lives ye led were mine.

—Rudyard Kipling

In recent years Gettysburg has been the scene of several re-enactments of some of the numerous battles that took place during July 1, 2, 3, 1863. They are usually "choreographed" by historians of the various re-enactment units that are to take part in the mock battle.

Most of the people who do re-enacting nowadays are serious hobbyists and pride themselves upon the accuracy of their "kit"—uniform or dress and accouterments—and their knowledge of the life in Civil War times. As a hobby it combines primitive camping and sleeping, cooking, and eating outdoors with the love of history.

It is a hobby to many of them in name only. Some spend thousands of dollars just to procure the minimum uniform or outfit necessary to portray life during the mid-19th Century. Those who have chosen to portray cavalrymen spend additional funds in the upkeep of horses, trailering, stabling, veterinary bills, shoeing and tack. The women who participate spend hundreds of hours sewing their own day-dresses and gowns, since that was often the way women actually produced clothing in a barely industrialized North and even less industrialized South in the 19th century.

Often when in camp—and nearly always when in "battle"—they remain true to their character, speaking in

Civil War lingo and talking of the last fight, of war news, and of war-related social events back home.

In 1981, on the 118th anniversary of the Battle of Gettysburg, a large reenactment was planned. During the last days of June and first sultry day of July 1981, re-enactors from all over the country converged on Gettysburg to live, eat, sleep, and "fight" near these hallowed grounds. Being the way they are, the re-enactors, as much to enjoy their hobby, were here to commemorate the brave men and women who sacrificed at Gettysburg to make this the nation it is today.

A friend of mine who is as serious a re-enactor as one can get, who, in fact, actually makes the reproduction uniforms from originals that he has studied, was participating in the mock battle of July 2,1981. He is a collector of original weapons, accouterments and clothing, and studies them almost under a microscope to make sure the clothing he reproduces is completely authentic. He is well known among re-enactors for his knowledge.

The day was incredibly hot and humid even for Gettysburg in July. The men were soaked to the skin and covered with grime and powder stains from the re-enactment. But, as uncomfortable as they were, they seemed to appreciate it since that was the way it was for their ancestors who fought 118 years before.

The day was drawing to a close and camp duties were over. My acquaintance and a comrade, still dressed in the uniform of Union soldiers, took a walk on the battlefield to cool off in the misty twilight.

They reached Little Round Top, the scene exactly 118 years before of some of the most savage fighting in the Civil War, now part of the gentle National Military Park where visitors come to ponder. They climbed the small hill and sat on the slope to watch the sun set magnificently over the South Mountains to the west.

*The west slope of Little Round Top
with the Valley of Death below.*

Perhaps there were some moments of contemplative silence between them as they looked out over the now peaceful valley between Little Round Top, and Devil's Den and Houck's Ridge. It doesn't take much in the cool evening, sitting on that historic hill to imagine scores of troops surging back and forth, leaving bloody heaps of bodies like gory footprints through the wheatfields and pastures. Through the valley—now named by someone who knew it well, the Valley of Death—meanders a small stream. Once called Plum Run, it was re-named after the battle "Bloody Run," for the few horrible hours in American history that it literally ran red with the blood of the men who were wounded and crawled to it for succor.

Being familiar with the battle, they probably could have named some of the men who fought there, on the slope before them, 118 years ago almost to the hour. No doubt they thought of Joshua Chamberlain and his rugged men from the rocky coasts and forests of Maine, who fought with the desperation of men in the last ditch—which is exactly where they were at the very end of the entire Union line—and died that way as well.

Looking out over the valley, perhaps they thought of old Lieutenant Colonel Bulger, commander of the 47th Alabama, silver-haired, shot and bleeding through the lungs and slumped down by one of the trees and left behind as his men were driven back. A young, upstart of an officer from a New York unit demanded his sword or he would shoot him. "You may kill and be damned," the old man wheezed, unafraid of neither the youngster nor that much older imposter, death.[1]

They could have remembered Confederate General Oates's comment that the blood stood in puddles in some places on the rocks. Looking just beyond Houck's Ridge, they may have seen in their minds' eyes courageous Colonel Edward Cross who, despite his week-long, recurring premonitions of violent death, still strode at the head of his men into the hissing maelstrom of the Wheatfield. His commander, General Hancock, perhaps noticing the black handkerchief tied bandanna-style around his head rather than the customary red one he always wore into battle, called out to him the promise of promotion: "Cross, this is the last time you'll fight without a star." "Too late, General," replied the morose colonel, already resigned to his fate, "This is my last battle." He was cut down to bleed and die amongst the rapidly reddening stalks of wheat.

In the distance they could see the Peach Orchard. Perhaps they thought of young corporal Thomas Bignall, Co. C, 2nd New Hampshire, who had, along with others of his company, been issued the hideous Gardiner's explosive minie ball. An artillery shell struck his cartridge box driving the 40 or so rounds of explosive bullets into his body and igniting them. For nearly half a minute his friends watched, horribly transfixed, as the bullets continued to explode within his quivering body in its prostrate dance of death.[2]

From the scrub brush just down the slope the two men heard a rustling and saw a soldier of the Federal persuasion emerge from the bushes on the rocky hillside and begin wearily climbing toward them amid the lengthening shadows and cooling air.

"Hello, fellows," he said with an excellent northern twang. "Mighty hot fight there today, weren't it?" My friend and his associate agreed as to the heat of the day as well as smiling at the authenticity of the man's kit. Sweat stained his indigo hat and black grime still blackened his mouth and teeth from where he had bitten numerous cartridges to pour their powder down the barrel of his musket.

They were about to compliment him upon his authenticity when he reached into his cartridge box and pulled out a couple of rounds of ammunition. "Here," he said. "Take these. You boys may need 'em tomorrow." He gave them a strange, wizened look, then turned and began making his way back down the slope of Little Round Top.

My friend and his companion watched for a few seconds as the stranger began his descent of the slope back into the evening. Rolling the cartridges over in his hand, my friend looked at them more closely, and remarked at the incredible amount of work it must have taken to produce such authentic-looking cartridges. They seemed to be original: Tied, folded correctly with just a hint of beeswax for lubrication, in every way seemingly an exact replica of Civil War era ammunition. Then he felt the minie ball inside each one. Re-enactors are forbidden by organizers and National Park Rangers to carry either ramrods or "live" rounds onto the field of a re-enactment for safety purposes, yet these contained the minie ball rolled within.

They looked down the slope on Little Round Top into the Valley of Death but could no longer see the soldier. A few yards down the slope he had simply vanished into the gathering, pale mists which at Gettysburg have that distinctive shape of long, strung-out lines of infantry mustered in formation.

My friend still has the ancient rounds of ammunition, treasured yet somewhat confusing mementoes of a small hole between worlds, a tiny glitch in the seemingly, but often illusionary, continuity of time.[3]

Slaying Days In Eden

...Three of these, college mates of mine.
What far dreams drift over the spirit,
of the days when we questioned what life should be,
and answered for ourselves what we would be!

—Major General Joshua Chamberlain

Gettysburg has changed a good bit since the first three tumultuous days in July 1863, when chaos held high court and the fields around the town were turned from nurturing corn and wheat to the planting of a much more valuable crop.

Gettysburg today, as it was during the American Civil War, is a small town trying to move ahead in time with concerns for its inhabitants' livelihoods and welfare. However, growth is and must be controlled more carefully than other small towns since there is so much hallowed ground in and around Gettysburg, sanctified by the blood and suffering of patriots from both sides who believed enough in their causes to die for them. Visitors from all over the world come to Gettysburg to try to understand this greatest of all human tragedies. Thoughtful people coming to Gettysburg are almost like petitioners going to confession: they come; they feel sorrow; most admit a profound shame for this Cain versus Abel play once acted out on a vastly more grotesque scale; their act of contrition over, they go home. We who live in Gettysburg must pay some of the cost for the continued cleansing of the souls of those who visit the fields of valor by carefully watching so that progress doesn't over-run them. There is even the feeling in those who truly love and appreciate the importance of these fields that those who allow or encourage such incursion of the profane onto the sanctified must someday sacrifice for their mindlessness of the past.

Yet growth is inevitable. At one time, the time of the Civil War, the dusty roads from Mummasburg, Harrisburg, and Carlisle all came together barely a full block north of the center square of Gettysburg—called in the 1860s, "The Diamond"—and just a hundred or so yards north of where the railroad ended at the depot. Now, of course, all that has changed.

Around 1860, Jacob and Agnes Sheads built their wooden frame house near what was then the end of town, probably hoping for the peace and quiet living at the edge of town would bring. Little did they know that the juncture of three main roads at their property would make their gentle home a focal point for the fiery emotions of soldiers heading to battle and the fearful despair of soldiers defeated, and of the personally traumatic emotions of one soldier in particular who would suffer and pass into the other world from the calm confines of their abode.

Carlisle Street ca. 1910 (Gettysburg Bicentennial Album, courtesy William A. Frassanito).

Some of the residents of Gettysburg who remained in the town after hearing rumors of the approaching rebel army heard a more ominous sound carry through the streets and alleyways early on the morning of July 1,1863. It started with a small crackle, a pop…pop…pop, pop…pop, coming from the ridges and roads to the west. Later they heard roars, great sheets of sound tearing in from the west and north. Soon, more soldiers dressed in blue came marching through the town, past where the Sheads had built their home. Some took the road to the left, toward Mummasburg; others marched straight out the Carlisle Pike; still others strode northeast, out the Harrisburg Road. Many of the soldiers spoke little English being of Germanic extraction, members of Major General O. O. Howard's 11th Corps. Perhaps some soldiers of the 11th Corps looked a little nervous at this, the very next battle after Chancellorsville, where Stonewall Jackson's men had driven them like sheep.

It wasn't many hours before Howard's men came tumbling back past the Sheads' house, some panic-stricken, routed once again from their contact with the enemy. Confederates were only a block or so behind them and shooting as they came. Any Union troops who attempted to make a stand—at the county poor house on the Harrisburg Road, or at Pennsylvania College on the Carlisle Road—were soon driven away by victorious Southerners. The entire Union line north and west of town had crumbled. As a South Carolina flag was planted in the Diamond, Confederates no doubt rushed past the Sheads' simple frame house feeling as if they had won Confederate independence. The small area around the Sheads' house, where three roads met, became a bottleneck of emotional energies as the hurrying troops—both vanquished and victors—all converged.

The Union dead and dying were scattered about like leaves and twigs after a windstorm. According to records, one poor Union soldier ended up at the Sheads' house, suffering through the stifling first two weeks of July until finally, mercifully, he died in the house on July 15.[1]

The years came and went. The town expanded, and the farm fields to the north of the Sheads' house began to fill with some of the larger homes in the area. The fields of fury north of the Sheads' house where men fought and ran for their lives were, after a few years, hardly recognizable to even the soldiers who had participated in the battle. The "battlefield" became the area a mile or so to the north, considered with each ensuing generation, to be beyond where the town ended. The people living in the houses had little realization of the emotional pain and physical agony once spilled out where they peacefully slept. Even the roads to Mummasburg and Harrisburg were re-routed to make room for the expansion of Gettysburg in the late 19th century. The College grew and changed its name from Pennsylvania College to Gettysburg College, in part to take advantage of the strange kind of fame the great sacrifice of men in battle brought.

The Sheads house changed hands a number of times. A title search shows that the property passed from the Sheads to one Hart Gilbert who willed the property to Jane Gilbert. She sold the house to Samuel Waltman and Emma his wife, in 1909. George Hemmler bought the house in 1921 and it stayed in the Hemmler family until 1942 when it was purchased by Morris Gitlin and his wife Ester. After Ester died in 1968, their daughter inherited it from Morris. The house eventually fell into the hands of an absentee landlord. They began renting to college students and the Sheads house became the temporary abode of groups of students that changed from year to year. It also seems to have become the permanent abode of some who come from a world unknown, and who remain, over the decades, unchanged.

Dr. Charles Emmons, Professor of Sociology at Gettysburg College, was gracious enough to open his files to me for both of my books on ghosts in Gettysburg. Dr. Emmons has written a fine cross-cultural study on ghosts in China titled *Chinese Ghosts and ESP: A Study of Paranormal Beliefs and Experiences* (The Scarecrow Press, Inc. Metuchen, NJ and London: 1982).

His studies show that there are many commonalities in the spiritual experiences between cultures. His students are encouraged to collect their own data and write about paranormal experiences.[2] Needless to say, they have a wealth of primary source material right here in Gettysburg. At least three students submitted papers that include the testimony of two different sets of women who experienced similar occurrences within the confines of the Sheads House.[3]

The data was collected first in the winter of 1979. Then, after the students moved out, data was again collected from several other students living in the house in 1983. The interesting part about this house is that two separate sets of data were collected, and the supernatural occurrences continued. There was no connection between the two sets of students except that they happened to live within the walls of the same house. The chronology is most important in that the individuals perceiving the paranormal events have changed, but the events go on. This is a pretty good definition of a "haunting" according to most sources. Therefore, I will emphasize the chronology of the collections.[4]

September 1979—The school year had just begun and a few of the women had moved back in after the house had been vacant most of the summer. The livable areas in the house provide three floors for occupancy. After hauling stereos and clothes most of the late afternoon, it was evening and two women who had just moved in to their downstairs rooms were relaxing in the semi-dark living room. Suddenly they heard the unmistakable sound in the dining room of glass breaking, as if a whole shelf of glasses had torn loose and crashed to the floor. They looked at one another quizzically. Neither of them remembered putting any glassware in the dining room that day. As they rose to get the broom and dustpan to clean up the mess, between the sounds of the cars moving up the dark street outside, they distinctly heard footsteps crunching on the broken bits of glass and moving slowly towards them. They bolted out the door and ran next door to get the young men who had also just moved in to their apartment for the year. Armed with baseball bats to protect themselves from the clumsy intruder, the men came running to attempt to confront the prowler who had either been hiding in the house while the women were moving in, or had slipped in while they were out at their vehicles. Cautiously they turned the corner into the dining room and flipped on the lights. To their surprise, no one was there. And, as well to their surprise, there was no broken glass to be found anywhere.

September 1979, one week later—A female friend who was left alone in one of the downstairs apartments told her friends that while they were gone she had heard some strange, distinctly loud, but indescribable noises coming from within the walls of the house and had felt cold flashes, even though it was still warm in early September.

November 8, 1979—One of the women was in the attic at 2:30 in the afternoon. She was alone in house, but heard a voice—as she described it—"say" to her the words "No, don't do it!" There was a pause, then "Stop!" She called downstairs to see if any of her housemates had returned, but she was answered only by the same voice yelling "Stop!" As if to punctuate the finality of the statement, and with the windows in the house closed to keep out the cool November breezes, two doors on the floor below her mysteriously slammed shut at that moment. Later, to one of the students who was investigating the story for his paper, she demonstrated that one door squeaks loudly when it is closed. She had heard no such squeak that afternoon. The other door, because of the high carpet, can't be blown shut by the wind, can be closed only with great force, and cannot be slammed without continued pressure on it.

November 11,1979—One of the women was napping in the afternoon. The shades were drawn and the room was in semi-darkness. She awoke to see what she described as a lady sitting in her rocking chair at the foot of her bed wearing a long, outdated dress with long sleeves and either short hair or hair done up in a bun. Though thoroughly frightened and confused at the appearance of a woman from apparently another century in her room, she gathered enough courage and found her voice long enough to ask the stranger a couple questions. "If there is anyone in here besides myself, knock twice for yes." Incredibly, from somewhere in the room she heard two knocks. "If you are friendly, knock twice for yes and once for no." No response. Growing frightened at the lack of an answer to whether the apparition was friendly, she repeated the first question and got the same response of silence. Suddenly, the image disappeared.

She sprinted downstairs, as her housemates described it, in hysterics. Our skeptical researcher discounts her story as merely the woman being half asleep, perhaps having a dream. And while that is possible, couldn't sleep—"death's counterfeit" as Shakespeare so poetically described it—be but one of the many windows to glimpses into the other world?

November 13, 1979—A third woman resident was sitting in the communal TV room. She was in the house with just one other housemate, yet they heard someone walking around upstairs and she suddenly shivered from a cold spot on the side of her chair. Their courage bolstered by one another, they managed to force themselves up the stairs to see if they had an intruder. They found no one. While on the third floor they heard what they described as papers falling, yet found no scattered papers anywhere throughout the house. One of the researchers says that one of the women claimed she had felt a hostile male presence staring at her. Apparently she is not the only one; all the women in the house at one time or another had felt that hostility.

November 13,1979—This appears to have been one of a couple of days and nights where a large amount of psychic energy was being expended. The resident who had seen the woman rocking in her chair was climbing the stairs to her room with her arms full. No one was near her on the stairs yet she felt someone tap her on the left shoulder blade three distinct times.

November 29, 1979—One of the women residents who had heard the glass breaking in the dining room saw a stack of papers float off her table, flipping like a deck of cards. Because of where the papers were stacked and where they fell, any breeze that might somehow randomly blow the papers in such an organized way would first have had to pass through a wall, through the woman herself and then across the papers.

December 9, 1979—One of the women who had heard footsteps on the floor above her in November, awoke at 12:30 A.M. after hearing a banging noise above her head. The woman who was tapped on the shoulder in November was also awakened by the same banging but another resident next door to the first woman was not awakened. The researcher checked out the house for animals, but the women said the noises—like the ones the guest heard coming from within the walls of the house—were far too loud for a small animal like a squirrel or mouse. During his investigation, the researcher checked to see if the noise had come from perhaps a tree branch slamming against the house in the wind. No branches were near enough to the house to even touch it.

On that same night the woman whose bedroom was in the attic had a little problem getting to sleep. In the darkened quiet of her upstairs room she heard someone walk from her third-floor window, around her bed and back again to the window. She couldn't describe what the entity may have looked like; she wisely kept hidden under the covers. The woman whose room was right below was also kept awake, not by one person walking but by what she described as an "army" marching in her upstairs housemate's room.

December 10, 1979—One of the women caught a sudden whiff of flowery perfume. She didn't recognize the scent as belonging to anyone in the house and no bottles were open or had spilled. (Dr. Emmons's marginalia records that others had smelled it too at one time or another.)

December 12, 1979—Finally, the women decided to pull out the Ouija board. All the women in the house agreed from feelings that they had that there were definitely two spirits and that they were of opposite sexes. The women, having had at least several experiences arbitrarily named their "ghosts" Agnes and Homer. (Interestingly, although none of the women had done research into the house, they coincidentally chose Jacob Sheads's wife's name.) Their first contact through the Ouija board was made upstairs: the name Ester was immediately spelled out. (Remember, none of the women had done any research, or knew about Ester Gitlin.) Through the board Ester said there were actually two other entities present and that one of the others was a woman and spelled out the names Steub and then Sterd. The women at the Ouija board also made contact with her ghostly companion but couldn't find out her name. Ester admitted to knowing Homer and liked him but said she was tired and kept spelling out "goodbye." The contact upstairs was broken.

The women took the Ouija board downstairs and contacted Homer. Through the board they learned that in life he had a wife whom he loved very much, but the marriage was flawed. His wife had had a lover, but apparently they had never been together in this house. Homer told them that he does not like women. He frightened the women when he said he was buried in Gettysburg. Quickly they asked if he was buried somewhere in the house. He answered, "no." Homer said he liked one of the women but not another. He said that even though he did not particularly like women because of his personal experiences with one in life, he was extremely lonely and liked the current residents' company in the house. Asked if Ester was his wife he responded she wasn't. Suddenly, the contact was broken, but they re-engaged for a time on December 30, and then again on January 4, 1980. Both resulted in short conversations. This was the last contact they were able to make.

No one knows the name of the poor Union soldier who breathed his last within the confines of that house and was probably buried temporarily in the yard, and then moved later to the National Cemetery in Gettysburg. If, however, his name happened to be "Homer," a sad and frightening insight into his life may have been gained by a rather unusual method this cold December night.

December 1979—Just before Christmas vacation two young female students who considered themselves skeptical of the ghost stories the residents had been telling were sitting near the Christmas tree in the living room. Suddenly they heard the doorknob to the exterior door being shaken violently. They jumped up and ran to the door. No one was there. No one was to be seen nearby.

January 2, 1980—One of the researchers was staying a little later after a party and was apparently alone after everyone else had either left or gone to sleep, when he heard footsteps upstairs early in the morning hours. (He could have shrugged it off as perhaps someone going to the bathroom, but recorded it in his paper, apparently because he wasn't convinced it was any of the women.) Some of the people who had been at the party returned and they began to tell ghost stories. The researcher said jokingly "Yeah, I feel a presence," when, as he described it, a "very odd sounding voice replied 'yes'." He couldn't distinguish the gender, but said it had an "echoey" quality about it. Six other people were present but only one other heard the ghostly reply.

January 6, 1980—Two of the women kept waking unexplainably throughout the long night. Subsequent research revealed that January 6 was the date of Ester Gitlin's death.

January 14,1980—One of the women who had heard the glass breaking when she had first moved in four months before was standing at the stove in the kitchen when she saw the reflection of a "black, bubble-like blob with a head" pass through the door of her room coming from inside the room. She turned around and checked the hall, but there was nothing to be seen. On this same day, one of the skeptics (perhaps, I should say, soon to be former skeptic) was walking down the hall returning from the bathroom. As she passed the first woman's room, she saw something out of the corner of her eye. She looked over her shoulder into the woman's room and saw in the doorway what she described as "an amorphous mass of white substance."

That same day—another one of those days with a great deal of paranormal energy being expended—the first woman mentioned above, and one of her housemates, were in the kitchen and heard furniture being moved in the section of the house above them. However, nothing had been stored in the small area; there was only empty space in the small room above the kitchen.

January 14, 1980, may have been the focus for an abnormal amount of psychic energy in the house perhaps because one of the researchers was there conducting an investigation. While in the cellar of the house he noticed a door bolted shut, and upon inquiry, was told by one of the residents that she had heard that the room behind the door was where séances were supposed to have taken place. Could other former residents have had strange experiences in the past and sought an answer? Could the "rumor" that séances took place in this inaccessible back room in the cellar be the last existing evidence of curious minds from the past attempting to understand the inexplicable?

One of the last events to occur in the house during the 1979–80 series of occurrences happened when one of the researchers was working with a Ouija board. Unfamiliar with the history of the house, he asked Ester what her last name was. It spelled out GISTWU. A six letter answer with three of the letters correct, if merely transposed. When asked the year she died, it spelled out 1896. Actually Ester Gitlin died in 1968. When asked if she was a man or woman, she responded "FEMALE" illustrating some creativity rather than merely answering the way the question was asked.

Finally, one of the women referred to an incident that seems to indicate a heightening of paranormal interference to a more physical level. Inexplicably, with no one around, her electric sewing machine would begin sewing by itself. The researcher checked the switch and connections, but everything seemed to be in order. But even after his inspection, the machine would continue, upon occasion, to start its sewing, the ghostly seamstress hard at work, but nonetheless, invisible.

A researcher in a 1983 paper mentioned a 1981 graduate who experienced some odd happenings the year she graduated. She and her roommates who all lived on the first floor, mentioned feeling a "presence around them" and of seeing a male apparition on the first floor. They also found the water running into the tub several times when no one had turned it on. At that time the researcher decided not to investigate what the second floor residents had to say because, he stated quite candidly, he was frightened.

January 21, 1983—The researcher began to interview the residents. They mentioned that they had found the heat thermostat set with sometimes fifty degrees difference from its original setting. An investigation by Dr. Emmons revealed that it took more force than just brushing by to change it. Dr. Emmons also confirmed that when he interviewed the first set of residents on Dec. 12, 1979, they too had had problems with the thermostat jumping up and down—something they had failed to mention to either of two previous researchers. As well, the loudness setting on the telephone kept being re-adjusted. Inexplicably, as if someone who was hard of hearing or perhaps was a great distance away were trying to listen to the conversation, the loudness setting would be set at its maximum when the students would pick up the phone. None of the students ever touched the loudness setting since not one of them had hearing problems.

One of the women had a frightening nightmare about a séance, only to find out that her housemate had been at a local pub that night discussing the house and séances that may have occurred in it. (Interestingly enough, there is a handwritten note on the paper from Dr. Emmons: "I think *I* told them at that conversation!" Obviously, he was there the night of the woman's frightening dream.)

That same day, January 12, 1983, the researcher found the courage to interview the residents of the second floor. Two of them related a story about being in one of their rooms and watching a tape literally levitate from a stereo speaker then propel itself across the room as if someone had lifted it and thrown it.

The women related how personal items have disappeared and reappeared in odd places in the house. All the women on the second floor admitted to having had nightmares about "orange blobish" figures pursuing them inexorably.

One of the residents, who lived in the front right hand room on the second floor, had felt a presence in the kitchen and, more frighteningly, next to her bed. The night before she was interviewed (January 11,1983) she said that her bed had been actually shaking for 15 minutes. She confirmed that it could not have been caused by a train. She has often smelled weird odors in her room. One night she said that she heard a strange, low moaning on the left side of her bed in the middle of the night. She was too afraid to even look in that direction until it stopped.

One morning around 3:00 A.M. she was awakened by the sound of a large number of horses trotting by the house for about 20 minutes. Peering cautiously out the window revealed nothing but the 20th Century street scene, devoid of traffic in the early hours. Dr. Emmons was told that some inhabitants had heard what sounded like an army marching by. Not unusual, considering that several thousand men had, at one time in that very space, marched by, devoted to death to the cause of saving their country.

One of the women related that she was near an air vent in the house when she heard a muffled voice emanating from it and felt a cold presence. Also, all the women spoke of the incredibly huge houseflies that seem to breed in the house. Perhaps they are attracted by the unexplainable, foul odors.

One woman also talked about a spot on the floor in front of her bed which often caused an odd burning feeling at the ankles. Two of the other women in the house confirmed the uncomfortable, searing heat as they stood barefoot in that same spot.

There is that theory beginning to emerge in the science of physics that encompasses the idea of the existence of parallel universes, both invisible to one another but existing side by side. The theory, while helping to explain some things, also raises as many questions as it answers. Is death simply a passageway to that other, coinciding universe? Could the house on Carlisle Street in Gettysburg, with supernatural occurrences so well documented by student researchers, and for some as yet unknown reason, be a window into this world's unseen twin?

Twice Hallowed Ground

Why, thou owest God a death.

—William Shakespeare,
King Henry IV, Act V, Scene i.

Gettysburg, with its lush farm fields, clear running streams and rolling hills drew good farmers from the eastern parts of Pennsylvania. In the 1830s and 1840s the influx was mostly hard working immigrants from Germany who disembarked in Philadelphia and began making their way westward. From the Lansdowne Valley they came to Lancaster County, and when the land was all sold up in Lancaster County, they went farther west, to York and Adams Counties to settle. Trostles and Weikerts and Hummelbaughs and Schmuckers, they were called "Dutch," a local aberration of "Deutsche." With them they brought their strongly independent religious beliefs as proselytized and propagated by Martin Luther.

The Lutheran Theological Seminary was established in Gettysburg in 1826. Originally the Seminary was housed in the brick double building still standing on the southeast corner of South Washington Street and West High Street. In 1832 it was moved to the brow of the ridge overlooking the town of Gettysburg from the west. Soon the ridge was christened by the townsfolk "Seminary Ridge" because of the large classroom buildings and dormitory which graced the gentle slope. They little knew how that name would be etched with the bitter acid of brotherly love gone bad into American military history or how that gentle slope upon which a school dedicated to teaching Christian peace would soon be christened again, this time sprinkled with human blood.

For years the Seminary matriculated those quiet souls who felt the special calling to the robes and pulpit. The languid summers came and went and the theologians journeyed to spread the word of God at large churches and small missions, to administer communion, to marry, baptize, and bury their parishioners as the seasons of life went around in their never ending circle.

But, in the summer of 1863 those mild summer breezes off the sloping fields near Seminary Ridge blew hot with the belligerent breath of great weapons and the agonized cries of countrymen at war with each other. The wheel of life's seasons seemed to groan heavily to a stop for three long days at the reaping time for death.

On the evening of June 30, Union cavalry commanded by General John Buford rode past the buildings of the Lutheran Seminary to bivouac a few hundred yards west on another of the crop-covered ripples called McPherson's Ridge. Buford, having ridden ahead of his men had seen Confederates that forenoon retiring from the fields west of Gettysburg. Being the kind of fiery cavalry commander he was, he knew they'd be back, and in force, and he would be there to hold them up until the infantry came.

He was right. The next morning Confederates came from the west and attacked his two brigades of troopers. Buford's men held out for over two hours, in part because they carried short, breechloading weapons called carbines that were issued specifically to the cavalry. They fought dismounted, every fourth man taking his and three others' horses behind the ridge to stand in safety. The men who did the fighting could crouch down or kneel or even lie down and still use the fast firing breechloaders. They made small targets to the advancing Confederates and stung them with their rapid fire.

But cavalry can rarely hold out for very long against veteran infantry. Gradually the troopers gave way, but not before the Union army's infantry was arriving on the field.

Buford had ridden back from his lines to the Lutheran Seminary and climbed to the cupola of the largest building—called "Old Dorm"—to look for the infantry. Squinting through his field glasses to the southeast, he saw the blue-coated foot soldiers of Major General John F. Reynolds, stretched across the undulating fields from the red brick Codori farmhouse on the road to Emmitsburg to the eastern base of the ridge upon which the Seminary stood. As he came down the ladder he was met by Reynolds.

"What's the matter, John?" said the tall, brown-bearded Reynolds.

"The devil's to pay!" was the irreverent reply in the structure more suited to vespers than oaths.

The situation to both men was obvious: Confederates by now seriously outnumbered the meager Union Cavalry and were lapping around their flanks. It was only a matter of time before Buford's line would crumble. Reynolds asked if Buford thought he could hold his line until the First Corps came up.

The feisty Buford seemed to bristle a little at the inadvertent challenge: "I reckon I can."

So off they went from the Seminary: Buford to inspire his exhausted horsemen to fight a little longer, and Reynolds to hurry his infantrymen along. For both, it would be their last big battle.

After several skirmishes and fairly wicked fights in the fall of 1863, the hard life of the cavalryman took its toll on the 36-year-old Buford. He died of illness in a Washington hospital a little over five months from his tenacious stand west of Seminary Ridge. And while Buford had a few months to live after his role in the Battle of Gettysburg, Reynolds had but minutes.

Reynolds, a 42-year-old native Pennsylvanian, probably felt a special commitment in fighting at Gettysburg. His own home lay only fifty-five miles to the east in Lancaster, and Confederates had already been reported at the Susquehanna River near Wrightsville. If the rebels were not stopped here, his own home and family might be threatened. Leading his men, not far from the McPherson family's farm buildings, he turned his head to the southeast to look for more of his brigades.

Somewhere to the west, just as Reynolds turned, a Confederate soldier pulled the trigger of his rifle-musket and the Major General took the soft lead minie ball in the back of the neck at something under 900 feet per second. The lush Pennsylvania farm fields, the thrilling sight of men marching to battle, the sounds of an army in combat all exploded into crimson nothingness for John Reynolds, and he entered the land where none of that matters. His participation in his final battle lasted only about fifteen minutes.

While his body was carried back to the town, his troops held out as long as they could. But pressure from the Confederates was too much, and by mid-afternoon the entire Union line, from the Fairfield Road northward to Oak Hill and over to the Harrisburg Road began to disintegrate. Seminary Ridge was abandoned by the Federal troops and occupied by the Confederates, and the buildings upon it became hospitals and operating rooms overflowing with wounded, suffering men and boys. No symbolic ablution was this for the sins of man in the fields of the Lord around the Seminary, but a real true blood sacrifice.

And, like every other building in the near environs of Gettysburg during death's horrible carnival the first three days of July that year, the large buildings of the Lutheran Seminary became shelters for the helpless and dying. Where penitents once knelt to pray, soldiers lay to bleed.

Reynolds was taken from Mr. George's small fieldstone house in the southern part of Gettysburg, where he had been lovingly carried by his aides, to his home in Lancaster to be buried. Though his body was gone, no doubt he—like thousands of others who felt their mortal bodies suddenly and violently torn from them—left energies to linger along Seminary Ridge and the long chain of the South Mountains which lead from it into Maryland.

Reynolds's military aides, upon examining his body, were surprised to find that his West Point class ring was missing. A subsequent search to find a West Pointer's most prized possession proved futile and they sadly assumed it had been lost in the frantic confusion of removing the general's body under fire.

Major William Riddle also noticed a small catholic medal around his neck. Odd, they thought, because the general was not Catholic. As well, there was a gold ring in the shape of clasped hands with the inner band inscribed, "Dear Kate."

The mystery was short-lived and when explained reveals a story overflowing with the human emotions of love, sudden grief, and sincere, deathless devotion.

The word of such a high ranking Union officer's death spread immediately. On July 3, while the battle that Reynolds helped start was reaching its fabulous climax, a note was received by the Reynolds family in Lancaster from a Miss Hewitt of New York. She had asked to view the remains. Jennie, John Reynolds's sister wrote that, "She seems to be a very superior person."

Miss Kate Hewitt, in her early twenties, was highly educated and from a fine, well-to-do New York family. As a young, single woman she traveled out west to work as a nanny. While there she met and fell in love with a tall, darkly handsome army officer named John Reynolds. Although he had been a bachelor for nearly four decades, the lovely Miss Hewitt's grace and youthful beauty were too much for the dedicated soldier: He lowered the ramparts to his heart and the tough professional officer surrendered for the first time in his life. The devotion was sincere and, as was soon to be seen, everlasting. Marriage plans were discussed; a honeymoon in Europe was planned. Then, with all the savage irony of a Shakespearean tragedy, the war came. He must go, he told her. He was a soldier, first and foremost. Would she wait for him? If he lived through the war, then they would marry. Certainly she would wait for him to come back, she answered with all her young heart. And if he didn't return...well, then she would join a convent.

True to her word, sometime after John Reynolds's violent death and mournful funeral, she moved into the Mother Seton Convent in Emmitsburg, Maryland, to become one of the Daughters of Charity. Not surprisingly it was the closest nunnery to, that most fateful of all places, Gettysburg. There is no record of her ever visiting the battlefield where all her dreams had been extinguished in one sudden instant, but in the spring of 1864 she was visited by Charles H. Veil, General Reynolds's orderly who was with him when he was shot, who had come to Gettysburg with Reynolds's sisters. He alone apparently made the side trip to Emmitsburg to visit the beautiful Miss Hewitt. In a remembrance he wrote that, "She made a great deal of me. I had to tell her all about the General, his last moments, and so forth, and she wanted very particularly to know if he left any last message...."[1] Sadly, the rebel bullet that took his life did its job with deadly efficiency. He left no final message to this world.

One of the last things she had told John Reynolds before he left her for the war was that if he should die in his country's service, the world would hold no interest for her. Perhaps that explains why she became very ill some time after Veil's heart-rending visit and had to leave the convent. She disappears from the records after that.

On July 8, 1863, Reynolds was to visit her at her home in New York. Instead, five days earlier, she visited him in his coffin after he had consummated another, more fateful rendezvous near the slopes upon which the Lutheran Theological Seminary stands outside Gettysburg. Instead of marrying his "Dear Kate," he took a more sinister and supremely jealous Bride in a union from which there is no divorce or separation.

Numerous stories abound of strange noises and odd creakings in some of the older Seminary buildings still sitting upon the ridge that bears their name. Krauth House has been known to produce post-midnight noises of large items being moved around and slid across the floor in the attic—moved, perhaps, by unseen orderlies and nurses to make room for even more wounded men to be jammed mercilessly in the stifling heat of an attic in summer, all of them not only invisible, but a century too late.

Krauth House on Seminary Ridge.

Books, being in abundance at the Seminary, were once used as makeshift (and no doubt uncomfortable) pillows for the wounded and dying boys who found themselves helpless to find better resting places for feverish heads. The sounds of books being thrown about the attic and slammed or dropped to the floor—perhaps by hands frustrated in this life by the weakness of wounded and torn flesh—have been reported awakening the students in the wee hours of darkness.

Having done research in the upper rooms of Schmucker Hall—now the Adams County Historical Society—I too have heard the strange groaning of floorboards above me while the volunteer caretakers of the building's archives were downstairs. Perhaps one of them had gone upstairs to walk the hall alone without my noticing it. Perhaps it was merely the old building after centuries of settling…just settling again. Perhaps not. Other historians have reported the phantom noises too.

Schmucker Hall—"Old Dorm"—on Seminary Ridge

A story floats around the Seminary that a chaplain from a branch of the military was staying in one of the dormitories—perhaps ancient Krauth House— and was told that he should remember to close the closet door in his room. It was through that door, the stories held, that the spirits would come. Perhaps he decided to prove that his faith was a bulwark against the incursion of spirits. Or perhaps he simply wanted to tempt the other world. Nevertheless, he left the closet door ajar as he retired. Later that night he was awakened, his breath catching at the strange creaking of the bedsprings and depressing of the bed next to him, as if some unseen weight just about the length of a reclining human, impressed itself in the mattress along side him.

In April 1992, a student at the Seminary who had read *Ghosts of Gettysburg* called and asked if I was interested in something that had happened to him and a friend just the month before.

He told me of how one night in the first week of March he had fallen asleep in his dormitory room in one of the newer buildings which sits on the west slope of Seminary Ridge just a few hundred yards or so from where the Union Army struggled on the first day of Gettysburg and John Fulton Reynolds spent his last moments on earth. About 2:00 a.m. he was awakened by a scream from down the hall. He recognized the voice as one of his friends, assumed that he was kidding around with someone in the dorm, and fell back asleep.

About 3:00 A.M. he was awakened by a cold chill. Thinking he had left a window open and that the wind had changed direction, he opened his eyes. Standing against one wall of the room leaning against his dresser was a man dressed in dark blue with a dark beard. At first assuming he was dreaming, he closed his eyes tightly and opened them again. The man still stood there, completely visible but only from the waist up. Fighting the growing panic, still hoping he was dreaming, again he closed his eyes and opened them. Still the man stood watching him. A third and final time, to assure himself he wasn't dreaming and perhaps to gather courage, he closed his eyes, opened them, and still the man stood, staring. The seminarian sat up in bed to confront the dark, bearded intruder, and the man vanished. Sleep came with great difficulty the rest of the night.

A day or so later he ran into his friend whom he had heard kidding around in the middle of the night and asked him what tomfoolery he had been engaged in to cause such a wild screech.

The friend proceeded to tell him that, at about 2:00 A.M. he had awakened to see a frightening and unexplainable intruder to his dormitory room. A man, darkly countenanced, had visited him through his locked door as he awakened, piercing eyes staring at him over a heavy, shadowed beard. What frightened him most is that no body accompanied the visage— just that veiled, disembodied face and head, floating surreally before him. While the head was completely discernible and distinct, the body just couldn't materialize itself. The scream his friend down the hall had heard was certainly not one of joviality, but of horror and fear.

Perhaps the most frightening thing about the story is that the dark, bearded man was alone, without a beautiful, charming young woman at his side.

A lost soul on his way to fulfill the sincere nuptial promises made earlier, now stuck meandering somewhere between Gettysburg, Lancaster, and Emmitsburg? Was it perhaps for her that he was searching? With so many souls set free on their fantastic journey within sight of the Seminary, who's to say for sure who might still be wandering, seeking…whatever.

But obviously, not finished with his nocturnal search, the dark-visaged apparition in indigo blue moved down the hall an hour later to seek further and pay yet another visit upon an unsuspecting student.

A Cavalryman's Revenge

No proposition Euclid wrote
No formulae the text-books know,
Will turn a bullet from your coat,
Or ward the tulwar's downward blow.
Strike hard who cares—shoot straight who can—
The odds are on the cheaper man.

—Rudyard Kipling

There is probably no other name more closely linked to the Confederate Cavalry than Jeb Stuart. He was the quintessential cavalry commander, leading his troops into small fights and big, making decisions that would affect not only the thousands of lives entrusted to him, but the fate of nations. His cavalrymen were, at one time during the war, not seemingly, but actually invincible, so completely dominating their Northern counterparts as to render them nearly non-effective. And Stuart himself played an important role by setting an example by his constant high spirits and utter contempt of personal danger.

The story of his military life is similar to those of so many of the young men who fought in that war: sincere friendships broken by politics and the accident of birthplace; anger at fate for stepping cruelly between classmates and family members; disgust at the destruction of places once held dear dictated by the necessities of war. For Stuart, his personal life, as well, was torn asunder.

He attended the United States Military Academy while Robert E. Lee was commandant, and graduated in 1854. While at West Point he got to know the likes of George

Washington Custis Lee, son of the Commandant, and Fitzhugh Lee, his cousin. Both would become Confederate generals. Alfred Pleasanton and William Averell were also at the Academy at the same time. They would eventually wear stars in the Union Army.

Stuart did well academically, but excelled at gaining demerits, especially for fighting. The odd thing about it, according to his classmates, was that he often got whipped, but was always ready for another good scrap. It was obvious that he just plain loved to fight no matter what the odds. It was a trait that in a few years—much to the chagrin of Pleasonton and Averell—would serve him well.

He was assigned to the Mounted Rifles after graduation and left for the frontier; while there he was transferred to the newly formed 1st Cavalry Regiment. In the regiment he counted as comrades-in-arms Joseph E. Johnston, John Sedgwick, George McClellan, Richard Garnett, and Lunsford Lomax. In the 2nd Cavalry Regiment, closely associated with the 1st, were Albert Sidney Johnston, Robert E. Lee, George Thomas, Earl Van Dorn, Kirby Smith, George Stoneman, John Bell Hood, and Fitz Lee. In all, between the 1st and 2nd Cavalry there would emerge in the coming conflict of the Civil War, two Union Army commanders, five full generals under Confederate arms, and over thirty commanders of brigades, divisions, and corps. They were men whom Stuart would literally bleed beside on the frontier, and later make bleed as his enemies.

While stationed at Fort Leavenworth, he met and married Flora Cooke, one of the three daughters of the commandant of the post, Philip St. George Cooke. There would be heart-tearing sorrow in that union, for while Philip St. George Cooke would remain with the Federal Army in the coming Civil War, and one of his other daughters would marry a Union officer, a third daughter would marry young Dr. Brewer who would become Surgeon General of the Confederate States Army, and St. George Cooke's son, John R. Cooke, late of Harvard, would become a brigadier general of Confederate infantry, get wounded five times, and eventually reconcile with his father—twenty years after the war. Of course, their most famous relative, James Ewell Brown Stuart—"Jeb"—would take his wife Flora, and follow the flag of the South while his father-in-law, although born a Virginian, would choose to command United States Cavalry, a position that would bring him face-to-face in battle with his son-in-law. His decision to command Union cavalry, invade Virginia and become Jeb's enemy said Stuart, he will regret only once—continually.[1]

Stuart's role in the Gettysburg Campaign has become a favorite sticking point with historians. Without ever analyzing the facts, most are happy just to accept the silly rumors and innuendo of past historians and even primary sources who had a reputation to defend, and continue to vilify Stuart, blaming his actions as some of the major reasons for the Confederate defeat at Gettysburg. Some go so far as to claim he was disobeying orders, and even that he was off chasing women instead of Yankees. The scoundrels offer not a shred of solid evidence.

Yet the controversy remains, and Stuart's ride from June 22, 1863, when he left Lee's Army to draw the Union Army's attention from Lee's invasion, until he rejoined Lee on July 2, 1863, at Gettysburg, is rife with agonized decisions and emotional turmoil. It remains, after nearly a century and a third, one of the most controversial aspects of Gettysburg. If the ghostly columns of gray cavalry do not still ride through the mists of the back roads of Virginia, Maryland, and Pennsylvania, certainly the emotional remnants of an exhausted four and a half thousand Southern cavaliers with the hopes, as well as the disappointments, of a nation pinned on them surely do.

Perhaps that is why there are some places along the route of Jeb Stuart where strange, unexplainable occurrences continue to happen.

Carlisle Army Barracks, 28 miles from Gettysburg in Carlisle, Pennsylvania, may seem too far away to be included in a book on the ghosts of Gettysburg. But aside from the fact that it held great emotional ties to Jeb Stuart and many of the officers under his command who fought with him at Gettysburg, there is indeed, at least one recurring link which, for a while, found itself back in Gettysburg frequently.

Carlisle Barracks ca. 1861
(Miller's Photographic History of the Civil War)

Stuart had approached the Carlisle Barracks during his ride to Gettysburg. There were a number of Union soldiers there and he didn't want it to threaten the rear of Lee's invading army which he knew to be in the area. In spite of the fact that as a pre-Civil War Cavalry training center it held special attachments for many of the men in the ranks with Stuart, because of military exigencies, he was compelled to set it to the torch.

Many of the barracks, where men like Fitzhugh Lee lived when he was instructor of cavalry, had to be burned. Stuart's own wife had lived at the barracks as a young girl when her father was commandant of the post. In fact, the daughter of Captain D. H. Hastings, Commandant of the post, was named Flora, after Stuart's wife. Stuart, before he ordered the burning to begin, spoke with some townspeople about little Flora.[2]

Stuart, according to the Stuart family, had visited Carlisle in October 1859, while he was showing off a device he had invented which facilitated a mounted-man's wearing of a saber. While many of the visitation records at Carlisle are sketchy (since many had been burned in the fires Stuart set and the pandemonium and looting after his departure) and his visit is not documented in writing, still it would make sense for him to display his device to the Cavalry Board of officers there.[3]

Other officers in his ranks as well held fond memories for the old post and barracks where pre-war friendships were forged. And, of course, even if they had never attended classes in Carlisle, they certainly had heard of the fine cavalry school there.

It must have been with great regret and sorrow that Stuart ordered the firing of the place that held so many memories for so many of his officers and was the childhood home of his wife. But there was a battle at Gettysburg to fight...

The barracks have been remodeled to accommodate not the spartan life of soldiers being trained for a career on horseback at the frontiers of the American West, but for the lifestyles of modem professional soldiers and their families. Where austere dormitory-style rooms once heard the pencil-scratchings of men figuring appropriate quantities of fodder and horseshoes for a staff ride, officers now key in to personal computers the logistics of freeze-dried Meals Ready to Eat, the number of armor-piercing shells needed, and the effects of wind-blown sand on thermal imaging devices. Almost every remnant of Stuart's burning of the barracks is gone.

It is a guarded qualification: Almost. It seems that someone or something is still not happy with Stuart's decision to leave the Federal Army he once pledged his allegiance to, and then burn the United States Cavalry Barracks at Carlisle.

Several years ago, I had the opportunity to work with Michael Gnatek, one of America's finest painters whose art graces the walls, in mural form, of the National Air and Space Museum in Washington D. C. His subject this time was Jeb Stuart. He produced, in colored pencil, a remarkable likeness of he great general and called it "The Last Cavalier." It was printed up as a fine art, limited edition print, and purchased by Civil War aficionados across the country. One who bought one of the prints was himself a soldier and was being sent to the prestigious school at Carlisle Barracks to further his studies in the military arts. With him he took his magnificent print of Stuart to hang on the wall of the restored barracks in which he was billeted.

Soon he was in Gettysburg at a local shop which did the framing of the piece. The framed print had dropped from the wall and the glass had smashed. But the circumstances were rather odd. The nails holding the print on the wall still remained in the wall; the strong wire behind the frame was intact; the frame itself was not out of line or damaged as it should have been had it dropped several feet to the floor; and the glass was broken in a strange way, pushed in, it seemed, by a force from the front. The people at the American Frame Shoppe in Gettysburg recently described it to me. It was like someone had lifted the print off the wall, set it down on the floor, and planted a heavy, booted foot on it, right in the middle of Stuart's image.

They fixed the glass and mitigated the scratches on the print as best they could. They returned it to its owner and thought no more about it...until he returned a few weeks later with the glass again smashed in the very same way. He explained to the framers the circumstances: again, the nails remained imbedded in the wall; again inspection revealed the wire well-attached; again the frame itself was undamaged; and again, the heavy smashing to the front of the glass right over the famous Confederate general's face. The glass was replaced, the print restored, and sent on its way back up to the barracks...only to return again a few weeks later, smashed.

This time the officer and his wife were awakened in the night by the sound of their print being broken. The sound was not the sound of a picture falling from the wall, but a popping, crunching sound, like a heavy foot on the glass. In the middle of the night he had gotten up to find, once again, that the image of the famous cavalryman who ordered the burning of the United States Cavalry Barracks at Carlisle had been desecrated. Again it was fixed and returned. Perhaps he was too embarrassed when (or if) it happened a fourth time to bring it back to the same frame shop; perhaps he was transferred from the Carlisle Barracks to another billet which proved safer for his much-loved print of the man who ordered Carlisle Barracks burned.

No doubt Stuart made enemies by his decision to burn the barracks. But for some loyal spirit—perhaps a former commandant and angry father-in-law—to hold a grudge for six score years waiting for just the right moments to avenge his old post, is indeed a study in eternal patience.

Lower Than Angels

All go to one place; all are from the dust,
and all turn to dust again.
Who knows whether the spirit of man goes upward,
and the spirit of the beast goes down to the earth ?

—Ecclesiastes

Not every apparition seen on the Gettysburg College campus can be associated with the college itself. Once again, anyone interested in studying what appear to be visions of individuals who lived in another lifetime must realize that the world did not look to them as it looks to us now.

During the Battle of Gettysburg, there were only three buildings on the Pennsylvania College Campus (which is what Gettysburg College was called prior to the notoriety the great battle brought to the name "Gettysburg") and they were in the general vicinity of where Pennsylvania Hall is today. The area to the north of what used to be the three buildings comprising the college was open farm fields out to the road to Mummasburg. There, along the roadside, stood a brick structure some call the toll house. It remains today, but it would take a great imagination to stand on the wide porch of the old toll house and try to peer through the houses and dormitories that have been built since the battle.

Glatfelter Hall is a magnificent brick edifice built in the late 1880s, with a classic, dark clock tower that seems to glower over most of the campus. The chimes bellow on the hour and, depending upon which way the wind happens to be blowing, can be heard around the north and west end of town.

The Glatfelter clock tower already has a reputation of being the site of a vision of a woman dressed in Victorian garb who can be seen floating back and forth through the openings in the bell section. The legend goes that, beautiful as she may appear and beckoning as she may be, it is unwise to climb the stairs in the tower to meet her. Broken-hearted by her betrothed's death in some unnamed battle, she leapt to her own demise from the clock tower years before. Like the ancient sirens, she is said to try and seduce young college men into climbing the tower and taking one last eternal step with her from the tower to the ground.

Jose Pimienta, in a study for Dr. Emmons, did some crackerjack research, speaking to college historians, librarians and archivists, and determined that no female student had committed suicide by leaping from the tower—or any other way—during the time period from 1888, when Glatfelter was built, and World War I. He covered two wars, and no grieving woman cheated the grim reaper for the lost love of a man. Still, there were those original sightings of the woman in the tower....

Glatfelter Hall and Stine Hall lawn.

Yet another story has arisen concerning Glatfelter which, considering the source, may have more credence.

The security people at Gettysburg College no doubt know more than some of them are willing to tell. Pinning them down is sometimes easy, sometimes difficult depending upon with whom you're talking. For Jose's paper, the onetime head of security at the college was very helpful.

He had an experience in the spring of 1971, and then another three years later, both at night as he was patrolling the campus and locking up Glatfelter.

He had completed his rounds through the majestic structure, locking all the doors to the outside, from the clock tower to the basement, and had been through every area shutting off lights to make sure no professor was working late. He had paused to use the restroom facilities before leaving and locking himself out. Suddenly, he was jolted by the deafening sound of chains in the hallway outside. He described the sound as very loud but short in duration. Rushing into the hall to see what it could have been, he was confronted by a set of wet footprints in a perfect pattern that ran across the hall. The problem was that there were no doors at either end of the prints: they entered the hall through one wall and left it through the other.

Three or four years later, he was parked in the college security vehicle, in the parking lot (now gone) of the old dining hall. It was approaching the end of his shift, about 5:20 A.M. on a cold, damp November morning. Early morning frost had settled in a fresh, hoary coat upon the land which, before the expansion of the college, had felt the cadenced shuffle of uniformed men at arms advancing to battle and then the broken hobble of the wounded as they made their way back from combat. The security man's eye was caught by a figure crossing the yard in front of Stine Hall advancing from where Plank Gym stands. A student out that early on a cold November morning might seem out of place, but not unusual, except for the attire. The officer thought he was wearing some sort of uniform—a postman's uniform, he said—but of gray, heavy material. The security officer saw white socks and only one dark glove on his left hand. But the man's gait was stuttered, a strange, uneven limp. He continued to observe the man make his way across to the middle of the dormitory lawn and then...vanish.

Perplexed at this totally unreal vision, yet with a police officer's professional curiosity to find out the facts, he left his car and walked over to the area. There, in the fresh frost before him were the uneven footprints of a person hobbling along. There could be seen the evidence, clearly cut in the white mantle, of a man's passing. And there, before him where the footprints abruptly ended in the middle of the snow-covered lawn, was the undeniable evidence as well of a human's sudden disembodiment.

We return to Pennsylvania Hall, scene of the unreal and accidental descent of two administrators late one night, into the Hades of a Civil War hospital somehow resurrected in the basement of the structure.[1] Over the years there has been the recurring sighting of what some have called "the signalman" in the Cupola of Old Dorm. A student of Dr. Emmons recorded a strange occurrence one October evening that adds one more witness to whomever is doomed to stand guard eternally above the campus.

As a first year student, the young man had been an avowed skeptic. Like all the students, he had heard of the ghostly sentry who walks his eternal post above the campus late at night, following long forgotten orders and adhering to a duty with a supernatural compulsion. He laughed off the stories, because, of course, anyone who believes in ghosts must be crazy.

Then, one night, the student was walking across campus to relax after a particularly hard evening of studying. It was late, about 11:00 at night, when the student was strolling from the circle just to the north of Brua Hall toward towering Glatfelter. He noticed that night the beautiful full moon and as he walked he heard what he described as a "rustling" above and to his right. At first he thought it was a bird, but was compelled to look up at the cupola of Old Dorm. There, to his amazement, he saw the blurred shape of a human, half hidden by the lower rails of the cupola and the trees. The image was a foggy white color and wore a hat. The student could distinctly see what appeared to be a dark rifle upon his right shoulder and a lantern being held in his left hand, and though misty in color he seemed to be solid. Blinking his eyes to make sure he wasn't seeing things, the student observed the ghostly soldier scanning the surrounding area as if on the *qui vive*, as all good lookouts should be. Then, suddenly, he began to peer in the direction of the student.

An icy chill ran up the student's back. Was he now suddenly intruding upon the other world? Had he accidentally crossed that thin essence that separates us from them? Whatever the realization in his mind, he felt for the first time that he might become a victim of the dangerous-looking weapon the soldier carried. He turned and began to run as quickly as he could back to his dorm. In a few short minutes, with that brief glance across the great chasm, he was a skeptic no more.

His roommates reported that when he got back to the room he had broken into a cold sweat, was pale, shaking, and visibly upset. Convinced by his demeanor of the sincerity of his confession to what he had seen, they decided to call some friends and return to Old Dorm to investigate. Perhaps gaining courage from numbers, the brave young man decided to go with them, but only after he was assured that from their window in the dormitory, no one was visible in the cupola.

As they crossed campus his fear was contagious: All were beginning to feel something strange under that full moon. They stood gazing up at the cupola when a security guard approached them to ask what was wrong. The young man told him of his experience and the officer recorded the information in his report book, seemingly finding the tale amusing.

"Old Dorm" now called Pennsylvania Hall
Photo Courtesy of Darlene Perrone

Then, as they all stood there, growing louder and louder in the deathlike silence of that evening, a horrifying, cold, unearthly wail cut through the moon-flooded night. They later described it as "high pitched, agonizing, and distinctly male," and lasting at least five long, blood-chilling seconds. On the battlefield where the rebel yell, a keen like the shriek of a banshee, once echoed among granite stained crimson, again it came to them across the centuries.

They all instinctively looked toward the cupola. They were convinced the horrible sound came from within the walls of Pennsylvania Hall. Amused no more, and convinced that what he heard signaled something completely out of the ordinary, the security guard called the Gettysburg Police Department for backup. When the other officer arrived, they searched the building together. The doors and windows were all locked. The entrance to the cupola was bolted shut. No one could have left the building without leaving a ground-floor door or window unlocked or without being seen by the several people gathered near Old Dorm.

The researcher verified all the facts later with the security office's records and was told one other interesting thing by the chief of security and his assistant: This wasn't the first time something of this nature had happened.

One doubts that it will be the last.

Castaway Souls

...alone I see this passing pageant,
—worn, thin hostages of the mortal.

—Major General Joshua Chamberlain

Jim Cooke and Davey Crockett, two morning deejays from a local radio station, called me just before Halloween 1991, to come on their program and talk about *Ghosts of Gettysburg,* which had just come out a couple weeks before. I did the show, read some stories and accepted phoned-in questions about the existence of ghosts on and around the Gettysburg battlefield. But more interesting than the experience on the radio was the invitation I received to accompany them—on Halloween, naturally—to two local houses in Gettysburg that were purportedly haunted.

The first was a local eating establishment and bed and breakfast, formerly a private home on Baltimore Street. While it remained a private home, the Civil War era house withstood numerous renovations to keep it in style with the changing times. The current owner has restored much of it to its quaint, 19th century appearance. It has become a Gettysburg landmark for outstanding food and exquisite Victorian ambience.

But being of the Civil War era, the edifice, like many Civil War houses in Gettysburg, contains more than just furniture and draperies, wall hangings and living people.

In fact, on sultry summer nights similar to those during which the battle was fought, the owner's daughter gives "ghost tours" of the house, relating to visitors the uncanny noises and the unassisted movement of objects about the rooms reported by guests. One visitor incredulously saw her small baby levitate from one of the beds, lifted by some unseen matronly hands, perhaps to be comforted—or perhaps for some other more sinister reason—before the infant was let down gently once again.

But Cooke and Crockett decided they wanted something more from their broadcast that morning. They invited renowned psychic Karyol Kirkpatrick to accompany them to the two "haunted" houses in Gettysburg and do some psychic readings.

Karyol has appeared on the "*Donahue*" and "*PM Magazine*" television programs and numerous times on local radio stations. She has helped several police departments solve "unsolvable" crimes, and at least half a dozen murderers are behind bars now because of her efforts. There was the phone call from a policeman on the car phone in a police van: He was transporting a body in the van to the local morgue. Over the phone Karyol described the body to him while she was hundreds of miles away. Every detail matched. The policeman listened patiently while Karyol described the deceased vividly, impressed—but not surprised—at her accuracy. He was used to working with her and her remarkable gifts.

Cooke and Crockett arrived at the house on Baltimore Street at about 6:00 A.M. The first thing they must do on all remote broadcasts is to tap into the phone lines in the house from which they are broadcasting. Walking up the steps to the house, Karyol started smiling. She felt that odd, familiar feeling upon approaching the house that the living weren't the only ones present and that her friends Cooke and Crockett were about to be treated to something strange.

Immediately the deejays had problems with the phone hookup. Pressed by a rapidly approaching airtime, they suddenly realized that every one of the several lines into the house was dead. No dial tone, no lights on the phones, nothing. They hurried to patch into a line in a nearby house. By then they were behind schedule, but Karyol had already begun to visit some of the rooms in the house and receive distinct psychic impressions in each.

She took notes, then came down to discuss her impressions over the radio. She had never been in the house before and knew nothing about what had transpired within the walls of the house during the savage fighting that occurred in the first three horrid days of July 1863.

Karyol had several distinct impressions while she was in the garret, but only one that seemed out of place. "Clay," she said. "Red clay," was an impression that come to her and brought confusion to many of us, until the owner's daughter told us that her father had discovered in his research that the Confederate troops stationed in the garret had been from Georgia. And while the distinctive red clay from Georgia had long before been worn from their shoes on the tedious march to Gettysburg, the homesick thoughts of some Georgia boys longing for their red clay farmland certainly must remain floating in that garret to this day.

Karyol also mentioned that someone was trying to get across to her the distinct impression that there was a traitor somewhere in the house and that he didn't want that traitor to give away their position. It only occurred to Jim Cooke later that, in this Confederate stronghold, by coincidence, all the men were wearing blue—blue shirts and blue jeans—and that their contact whom they kept calling back at the station, had a radio moniker of "The Captain."

It was time to move on to our next "haunted" house. Still the phone lines into this house were dead, as they had been since our entering it. Karyol and Davey had gone into the kitchen when he suddenly came running out and waved to us. "You've got to see this!" he said. As we jammed into the kitchen, Karyol was standing about five feet from the telephone on the wall. As she drew to within a foot or so of the phone, the LED lights on the dead phone suddenly went berserk, flashing up and down like a Christmas tree. She backed away and they stopped. She approached the phone and they started again. Then, suddenly, only one light, the one signifying "intercom"—meaning someone within the house—began flashing.

Karyol reached for the handset and picked it up. The flashing stopped, but no one was on the inoperative line. She hung the phone up and the intercom light began flashing desperately again. The lines were still dead, but someone within the walls of the house still wanted to communicate with Karyol—someone they perhaps knew would be sympathetic to their pleas.

She picked up the handset again. The flashing stopped and she listened. Again, no audible voice. Karyol closed her eyes and began talking. "You're trapped in the past. You're not needed there anymore," she said eerily. "Walk toward the light. You don't have to be a soldier anymore. Walk toward the light." She hung up the phone.

I asked her if she had heard anyone on the other end of the line. Karyol shook her head no and, pointing to her head, said that she'd heard him up here, inside. Suddenly the intercom light began flashing again. Everyone in that kitchen, from the owner's daughter to the deejays, to the cook, to myself, was flabbergasted at the persistent flashing, the desperation with which this poor lost soul was trying to communicate with one he knew was sympathetic and who could guide him from his entrapment.

Again she lifted up the receiver; again the flashing stopped; again she spoke to the spirit imprisoned in a time long past, of being able to free himself if he only tried, of walking out of the abhorrent darkness toward the light so often described by those who have had near-death experiences. "Walk toward the light."

But by now we were in a hurry. Cooke and Crockett had to move their equipment to the next house and prepare to broadcast. This unexpected brush with an unseen resident of the house had held us up. Yet, as we left the kitchen I looked back to see the intercom light flashing yet again in a desperate, lonely plea for release from an invisible spiritual prison.

The Jennie Wade House is located at the edge of Gettysburg on the road to Baltimore. Actually there are three houses in Gettysburg associated with the young woman who would gain dubious fame through the odd circumstances of her single death during the three days in American History when death reigned over a small, fetid kingdom. There is the house on Baltimore Street where she was born; there is the house on Breckenridge Street where she lived; and there is the house at the edge of town, never owned by a Wade but rented to her sister, where she came to die.

The facts surrounding her death are basic: She was in the wrong place at the wrong time. Compelled by sibling love to take care of her sister who had just given birth, she had temporarily moved into the house before Union and Confederate maneuvering placed it between their lines. Compelled also by the eternal pleadings of hungry soldiers, she was at her dough tray about 8:30 in the morning when a stray minie ball penetrated two doors and struck her in the back.

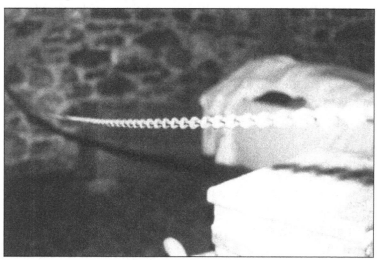

The Jennie Wade House

Yet the rumor and innuendo about her life and family continue to this day, whispered and giggled about, but with very little substantiation. However, it appeared to Karyol and at least five others that morning, that someone associated with the Wade family was still not resting easy, vexed still after years of icy eternal sleep.

That the Wade family was not well-off was common knowledge around Gettysburg in the decade before the Civil War. That the family was destined to struggle through hardships fated to be upon them now seems true. What the weird winds of time would do to disrupt even their memory was still to be seen.

Jennie's father had been convicted of larceny and sent to prison when she was 7-years-old. How prison life twisted him is evident: When he came home two years later, his wife was compelled to request the court to declare the former tailor insane. Off he went to the Adams County Alms House and left the family without a provider. Mrs. Wade and her daughters Georgia and Virginia (Jennie), took up the tailor business, probably raising some Gettysburg eyebrows in the process: Victorian women just didn't run businesses; that was for the men. But the three women had to put food on the table for themselves and the three little boys in the family, and so they endured the whispers.

And while the moneyed ladies of the town talked, the young Wade girls went on with their lives. Georgia married Louis McClellan—a Gettysburg boy already a soldier for the Federal cause—in 1862. They rented the north half of the house on the Baltimore Road where soon Georgia's sister would die.

Jennie was apparently in love with a childhood playmate, Johnston Skelly, known to all in Gettysburg as Jack. I say apparently because fate intervened before any public announcement could be made. But there is evidence: Found in the apron pocket of the girl upon her death was a photograph of handsome Jack Skelly, his image carried close to her even as she baked bread. It is almost certain the two had a relationship deeper than just friendship, yet that too would be marred with vows broken by destiny and an irony only death can orchestrate.[1]

Some say they were engaged to be married, but that is a question that will remain forever unanswered. It took three deaths to silence the truth.

Jack took a bullet in the battles around Winchester, standing in battle line with his other friends from Gettysburg who wore the blue on June 15, 1863, in one of the dozens of fights that occurred during the month-and-a-half long Gettysburg Campaign. Lying wounded and helpless, dying as a prisoner of the rebels, he was surprised to see at his pallet an old friend from Gettysburg, Wesley Culp, in the uniform of the South. Wes had gone to Virginia before the war to follow his employer, and when conflict broke out, he stayed with the Virginia militia unit he had joined. Fate threw his unit against his boyhood playmates and then brought him face-to-face with his own past as he knelt next to Jack's dying form.

It is said that a deathbed request was made: If West ever made it back to Gettysburg, would he find Jack's sweetheart and deliver one last message. Of course Wesley Culp agreed to his friend's dying wish. He would find Jennie Wade and deliver the missive.

Killed in the early morning hours of July 3, 1863, on the hill that bears his family name, Wes Culp was buried, his body lost, and Jack Skelly's message with it. Not that it mattered. The would-be recipient of the message, Jack's sweetheart Jennie, lay cold in the cellar of her sister's rented house, by then unable to hear any more earthly words of love, forever.

The deejays had set up in the Jennie Wade House and Karyol had been visiting the rooms, getting impressions and jotting down notes. Bob Wright, Assistant General Manager of the Jennie Wade House Museum was with them. Karyol had never been in the Jennie Wade House before and, as with her visit to the other house, was told nothing about the history of it. The taped narration was not on while she visited, and so any information about the Wade family tragedy was unknown to her. They moved through the house, generally following the same journey Jennie's lifeless body made as Union soldiers carried her from the kitchen upstairs, through a shell-hole in the dividing wall and into the other half of the house, then downstairs and into the cellar, the safest place in the house from the battle that still raged about them. There they laid her on a makeshift bier in the corner of the cold stone cellar, the family huddling in the claustrophobic damp, keeping their macabre vigil, mostly in shock, next to the body which moments before had been vibrant and moving, now releasing the vital spirit which was Jennie Wade.

The cellar has since been a place of uneasiness, even fear. Many visitors to the house, after paying their entrance fee and touring the rest of the house, will refuse to descend into the makeshift mausoleum, or, once there, will hurry out before the taped message is through. Video cameras, while working well enough just outside the cellar, will record nothing once below ground level. Karyol Kirkpatrick felt an unusual presence there, something she described which possessed the emotion of something left undone—a mourning unfinished perhaps, she suggested.

Considering the three souls tied forever together in an eternal quest to deliver a last message, the uneasiness concentrated in that temporary subterranean tomb is understandable. Yet Karyol also mentioned, rather casually, something about a father. A father, she said, who had not been allowed to mourn properly.

The group began to ascend the stairs to the sunlight. Bob Wright, the manager, was the last to leave with Karyol just in front of him. From the first step she turned and glanced back into the cellar, her eye drawn by some movement. "Oh, look," she said to Bob, pointing across the room at the small chain that ran from a pillar to the stone wall across the cellar, separating the area for visitors from the spot where Jennie had lain in state. "I think it's Jennie's father," she said matter-of-factly, "He's trying to tell us something."

As Karyol and Bob stood there in the dark cellar, the chain began to sway back and forth, with no one near it, with no one visible having touched it. For a full minute it swung as the rest of the visitors to the house clambered back down the stairs to see this physical manifestation of some spiritual uneasiness.

The chain's movement was odd: It swung as if it were a solid piece of wire, or as if each link were attached to one another, or as if all points on the chain had been touched at once. (Subsequent examinations by Bob and Dr. Charles Emmons, the Gettysburg College professor who wrote a book on ghosts, showed that even during the busiest times on Baltimore Street, the heaviest trucks failed to produce any movement in the chain. As well, when Dr. Emmons touched the perfectly still chain in my presence, the movement was of the wave variety, clearly visible running back and forth along its length, and not the solid movement he had seen before.) And when the chain stopped moving the first time, it slowed far too quickly to allow for simple momentum: something unseen had stopped it.

Jennie's father, John James Wade, Sr., died in 1872 in the Alms House, his mind still not able to cope with the realities of this world. Perhaps it is from the Other World that he is finally allowed to mourn the passing of the daughter he lost, first when she was seven, and again when she was twenty.

Off-Off Broadway

There are more things in heaven and earth Horatio,
Than are dreamt of in your philosophy.
—William Shakespeare, *Hamlet, Act I, Scene v.*

Most people who visit Gettysburg are under a misconception as to where "The Battlefield" actually is. The monuments and markers for the most part, delineate the battlelines of the two armies. They stretch down the two major ridges once splashed with human blood—Cemetery and Seminary Ridges—and in a wavy arc a mile and a quarter west and north of town where fighting occurred on the first day. The United States Government owns much of the land, or at least the right of way where the monuments stand, along these major battlelines. Many visitors to Gettysburg ask the question, "Where's the battlefield?" expecting, perhaps, a fenced-in area they can see with one sweep of the eye.

While the government owns or has right of way to some 6,000 acres, "The Battlefield"—where close to 175,000 men fought, maneuvered, were wounded, bled and died—must cover several hundred square miles. Nearly every road from Chambersburg to Carlisle to Harrisburg to York was crossed and criss-crossed by cavalry, and infantry marched a good bit of that area as well. The web of roads between the small towns were all covered too. You can hardly drive along a road in Adams County, York County, Franklin County and Cumberland County that, at one time, wasn't used by the two armies. Fights and skirmishes associated with the world famous Battle of Gettysburg occurred in towns with hardly recognizable names like Fairfield and Hunterstown, Carlisle and Wrightsville and Hanover, Monterey Gap and Zora and Cashtown.

So, the answer to the question, "Where's the battlefield?" is: you're standing on it. Whether you're in a modern motel lobby or sitting in a Gettysburg resident's fancy dining room on Broadway, you're on a part of the Gettysburg Battlefield, probably in the same space (but at a different time, of course,) where men struggled, or charged, or retreated, or perhaps were wounded, or died.

And Gettysburg has expanded from the somnolent, dusty village centered around a crossroads established for farm commerce containing about 2,400 souls, to the small, busy town it is today of about 8,000 people. After the great battle, in the 1880s someone discovered that the hilly land a few miles north and west of Gettysburg was perhaps the finest soil God ever put on earth (or 50 at least in Pennsylvania) for growing fruit trees. An industry was born, and Gettysburg grew a bit to accommodate it. Someone also realized that, even after the soldiers were gone and the Civil War was softening into a musty but still horrible memory, people— Americans, Europeans, Asians—eventually by the millions, were drawn in an unexplainable way to visit this place of vast human carnage to ponder the reasons why men did what they did here, and to scrutinize and study and eventually wonder what good could be found in the suffering of one generation for the sins of others. Gettysburg again grew, and continues to grow, to accommodate another industry, this one of tourists of the heart and explorers of the American conscience.

And, of course, Pennsylvania College (which sometime after the battle changed its name to Gettysburg College since people just wouldn't quit calling it that) grew and expanded, adding buildings and staff who needed housing. So some of the fields that once thundered to thousands of marching men were eviscerated for cellars and foundations.

Martin Winter, a local insurance agent, was responsible for most of the development of Gettysburg to the east and north during the first decade of the 20th Century.[1] The fields to the north, of course, were the scene of the Union retreat—actually a rout—after their defeat on the first day of July 1863. Men crossed those fields in desperate, panic-stricken haste to escape a pursuing enemy. They were shot in the back and brought down with shrapnel whipped into their legs as they tried to run. It must have been like one of those dreams we've all had where something evil and life threatening is approaching us and we cannot run, our lower limbs being suddenly and inexplicably leaden. Except this, for the soldiers, was their own horrifying reality.

Winter purchased the fields of war, subdivided them, and sold them off to people of apparently substantial means; most of the houses on Lincoln Avenue and Broadway, about three-quarters of a mile north of the square in Gettysburg are large, well-designed, and attractive structures, many of classic architectural designs.

So the small hills and ridges you see today north of Gettysburg when you visit are indeed the fields of carnage—"the Battlefield" all seek. And where the many lovely homes lie north of town were also the spots of untold suffering and heartbreak, of families broken apart by the sudden, swift death brought by a minie ball or other fragment of whistling ordnance. And it seems that some of those who fought and died in the fields whereupon spacious homes for the well-to-do were built—and even some who never fought there—are not quite satisfied to repose in the supposedly eternal rest of the ages.

One lovely, well-kept home on Broadway seems to demonstrate the fact that not everyone is susceptible to visitations by apparitions, even when they legally own the house where the spirits are supposed to reside.

The owners say that they think the home was built between 1917 and 1920. They themselves have never been witness to any strange happenings, but the woman who lives there said that relatives have seen some odd things go on within the walls of the elegant home on Broadway.

Her mother was visiting and using the guest room on the third floor of the house. Everyone had retired for the evening, which passed quietly enough for most in the house. But the next morning, after her husband left for work and the children were packed off to school, the woman listened to her mother tell her a story that hardly seemed believable.

It seems that she was awakened in the middle of the night by the appearance, entering from the dormer window on the third floor, of two strangers who seemed to float toward her bed. Incredulous, the woman's mother still maintained enough equipoise to notice details of the couple. One she described as a female child, looking to be about ten years old, with golden-blonde ringlets—"Shirley Temple curls" she called them—who stood hand-in-hand with a man dressed entirely in black, almost as if he were in mourning dress. The woman's mother said that she got the distinct impression that they were father and daughter. They stood together at the foot of her bed and looked at her. As if they had entered the room merely to see who was staying overnight, slowly they turned and began to move toward the hallway. The door to the hallway didn't open; it didn't need to. They simply walked through the wall.

Although never having had an experience with an apparition in the house, the woman certainly believed her mother when she told her that morning so matter-of-factly about the odd visitors to her third floor bedroom the night before. And her belief—even without ever seeing the spirits—must have been solidified even more within the next year or two after hearing of the experiences of two other family members who stayed on the third floor.

Her sister was visiting and staying on the top floor. One morning she described a strange experience. Though alone on the third floor, she looked into the hall and caught, out of the corner of her eye, the figure of a man heading down the hall toward the stairs. The owner's husband had already left for work and so the male presence in the hall was, and remains to this day, unexplainable.

The owner had her interest piqued one more time in recent years. Another family member, an aunt, was staying over, once again on the third floor. Again, the morning coffee was mixed with a tale of a man who simply appeared out of nowhere in her room, stood looking at her for a while, then vanished.

One of the more striking houses on Broadway is a large gray stone house at the end of North Washington Street. Built in 1930 by Dr. John McCrea Dickson, after his death in 1939, it was willed to his wife Marion. After her death in 1971 it was sold to the brotherhood of Sigma Nu Fraternity at Gettysburg College. From the north windows one can see out over the fields of battle that were littered with so much carnage on the first day's battle at Gettysburg. The monuments to the hundreds of men and boys who fought and were crippled or slain on the fields to the north are visible only a few hundred yards from the house. Yet with all the spiritual energies extinguished within view of the site of this house, the residents unexplainably—and perhaps a little unfairly—continue to blame poor Dr. Dickson for the poltergeist activity that occurs frequently within the solid stonewalls of the edifice.

One of the students who had interviewed me years ago for research on local folklore and had written a paper on ghost stories on the battlefield was a victim of the poltergeist in the stone house, yet never included it in his paper. Instead he told it to another individual who included the story in his college thesis.

West Broadway

It seems that one night in 1978 he had been studying in one of the larger rooms in the house. It was what the brothers called the "five man" room but the student was alone at the time. Suddenly the door to the room opened, shut, and then opened again. Obviously, one of the other brothers was behind the door playing a trick, so the student got up from his work and walked into the hall to confront the jokester. But there was no one in the hall, and no way anyone could have played the prank and gotten away between the time the door opened the last time and the student reached the hall. As he turned to walk back into the large room, the lights went out. Thinking it an odd power failure that darkened just the one room, he walked to the light switch to test it and…the lights turned on normally as he flipped the switch. Perplexed at all the strange activity, unable to relegate it to reason, but unwilling to accept that something truly paranormal was happening, he returned to his desk and sat to try to resume his studies. Without warning, a large glass mug was thrown—"thrown" according to the student's own report;

not "fell" or "dropped"—from the shelf where it had rested, to the floor of the large room, completely missing, on its way down, a table directly below it.

Another brother reported lights going on and off by themselves one early morning in 1978. He had just pledged the fraternity and had been studying in the house much of the night, and began hearing what he described as loud noises as well…noises that apparently no one else in the house heard.

Finally, two students were staying alone in the house over a college vacation break. It was a rainy night. One of the brothers was on the third floor and the other was downstairs. The one who was downstairs heard the front door open and the unmistakable sound of someone shaking off a wet raincoat. He heard footsteps begin to ascend the stairway. Curious, and a bit cautious as to who might have entered a private fraternity house, he began to follow the sound of the footsteps at a discrete distance. He listened as they went all the way up to the third floor where the other fraternity brother was sitting. Expecting to find two people on the third floor, he was incredulous to find only the one brother who said that, as the first brother was engaged in following the distinct sounds of a mysterious stranger up the stairs, he hadn't heard a thing.

A woman whose husband was employed by Gettysburg College brought their family to Gettysburg and moved into one of the beautiful Queen Anne style structures on Broadway. Research done by historian Elwood Christ in 1989 indicates that the house was built around 1901, but the lot, like all the lots Martin Winter marked off was part of the land that dates back to the famous Manor of Maske, an immense tract cut from the original William Penn Grant. The house sits (as do most of the buildings in the northwest corner of town) near where the road once known as the Shippensburg Road cut through the fields and junctioned with the Harrisburg Road and the Carlisle Road about a block north of the railroad station. The road, of course, predates even the town of Gettysburg, having been "confirmed" in 1769–1770.[2] Perhaps, not surprisingly, it struck the main east-west road near the spot where Samuel Gettys had established his fine tavern as a rest stop for travelers from Shippensburg to Baltimore or Philadelphia.

Within the first year of moving into the house, the woman had strange feelings as if someone was behind her staring. We've all had those of course, but when we turn around, usually there is someone there. But when she turned around she saw nothing...at least at first.

She is a night person. She often worked late, after the rest of the family was in bed. The uncomfortable feelings of someone staring at her continued, especially, she noticed, whenever she had her back to the door into the library. And the feelings grew more intense, gradually changing from a slight realization that someone might be behind her, to the strange fear that eyes were indeed upon her, to a distinct, shiver-inducing chill.

The feelings were not new to her. As a child growing up in the South, she and her sister, who shared the same room, would hear, in the middle of the night, footsteps begin in their living room, walk down the hall, enter their bedroom, and stop at their beds. Of course, as they listened and watched while the steps approached, no one was there to make the sounds. It wasn't until they were grown up that their mother told the girls that an elderly man had died in that house before they moved there. You can imagine how surprised their mother was when the girls told her that they had been visited by someone fairly frequently over the years who could be heard but never seen, who apparently had some special attraction to the house, and in particular, to the young—and very much alive—children abed there.

But the feelings she had as an adult in Gettysburg had a more frightening effect. They continued to become more intense, until finally one night, unable to take the uncomfortable feeling of eyes boring into the back of her skull and the intense cold in the middle of the summer, she was driven to rise from her chair where she had been working late, and rush upstairs. She had turned out all the lights except for the small one which lit the stairs. For some reason, she stopped on the stairs, turned, and looked back at the door to the library. There, in the doorway to the darkened library, was a tall column of distinctly blue light, glowing. She turned and sprinted up the rest of the stairs.

It was several days before she could bring herself to work late again. With an odd combination of needing to finish some work late at night and an almost morbid curiosity to perhaps again see that odd blue columnar translucence, she began to work her late night hours once more, alone on the first floor. She expected to feel the chill, or turn around to see the strange, electric-blue phosphorescence in the doorway to the library. She expected it, but for a while, nothing happened.

Then, once again, just after midnight, her tranquil work was pierced by the same strange feeling of being watched, and the odd, numbing chill wrapping her. The feelings were uneasily familiar, and she hurriedly finished her work, turned off all the lights but the one in the stairway, and rushed to the stairs. As if compelled, she stopped—not really wanting to—and looked down the stairs to the doorway into the library.

There it was again. The column of blue light stood in the doorway. Perhaps she remained staring at it a little too long, for as she watched, it slowly began to leave the library door and come toward her. She flew up the stairs to the safety of her husband and the warmth of her bed.

In the daylight things seem so reasonable, so commonplace. Lights that appear and flash across the ceiling can be explained as sunlight reflecting off car windshields. Colored lights within a house can come from the sun shining through a blind. A blue light can be merely the daylight entering through a piece of stained glass in a window. A six-foot high, 18-inch wide transparent column of animated blue light, which seems to move in intelligent response to the actions of a human being can certainly be explained...

And deep into the night those logical explanations should hold true. Shouldn't they? The woman, of obviously superior intelligence, would make peace with what she saw in her own mind, place it behind her desire to finish the work ahead of her, and, within a few nights, be back working late. She returned to her work, and, of course, it appeared again.

For a third time she felt the eyes staring through her, the chill wrapping itself about her from behind like an unwelcome lover's arms, and the heavy presence of another being in a related space. Out went the lights. Up the stairs she strode quickly, only to stop and turn once more to see the ghostly azure column float from the doorway of the library toward her before she bolted up the stairs. To this day she says she thinks whatever it was just wanted to make sure she was truly leaving its area.

For a while she couldn't work late anymore. The further away we get from an event in time, the better off we are. The memory has a tendency to lose all the gravel and scabs and fears of even the most recent past, so that we can get on with our lives. So it was.

But then a colleague of hers needed a long dissertation typed. Again she set up her little office in the dining room and went to work. Nearly every night for two weeks she worked while the others slept, usually after midnight when everything on Broadway in Gettysburg was quiet, and sometimes as late as two o'clock in the morning. She was approaching the end of the dissertation when the eerie, unexplainable sounds started.

They began with a slight rustling of papers in the library. Absentmindedly she called out to her husband; perhaps he had awakened, had silently descended the stairs and was looking for something. No one answered.

More rustling. And creaking. What was going on, she thought, and walked to the library to see which of the children had gotten up. Nothing. No one was in the library. She returned to her typing.

Minutes passed and she became absorbed in the final touches on the manuscript. The rustling of papers in the library started again, louder this time. More creaking of the chair, and of the wooden floor. And footsteps.

Determined to finish her work, afraid to go back to the library or even look at the door, she continued to type. The noises in the library got louder, building upon one another: papers rustling, crackling, being crumpled, the groaning of the old chair and the even older floorboards, books falling, and the footsteps hurrying about in an ever increasing rush toward pandemonium. She finally stood, being able to take no more, and ran to the doorway, fully expecting to see the library ransacked. As she touched the doorway, the noises ceased. As she peered cautiously into the room she saw that not a thing had been moved, not an item had been touched. The room was unchanged.

Having only a few pages left in the manuscript and with quietude descendent again upon the house, she returned to the typewriter. Looking at the clock she saw that it was two o'clock in the morning, almost time to stop work anyway. She would force herself to finish this last page, then climb to the sanctuary of the second floor. She had only been typing a few minutes more when she felt it.

Describing it just recently she said it was not like the other times where she simply felt a chill, or felt surrounded by the cold. This time it was the strongest feeling ever, an oppression, as if there was "something over me," like the heavy, dark, chilling blanket of death thrown upon her.

She turned to see the familiar blue column in the library doorway. But this time something was different. This time she noticed, to her horror, that it had distinct features.

The "Ghost in the Blue Column"
drawn by the woman who saw him.

She saw a man standing within the blue column, his hands on his hips, legs planted defiantly apart. He had on a pair of tight riding breeches and high boots. His shirt had puffy sleeves. He had a full head of hair, which hung down over his collar in the back. He had no moustache, but instead wore mutton-chop whiskers, of the variety so popular during the mid-19th century. His head was twisted at an odd angle, she said. He was "not unattractive." And he wore upon his handsome face, an odd, puzzled, angry look, as if he were about to say, "What are you doing here? How did you get into my world?"

It took her less than a second to realize what she was seeing and exclaim in fright, "Oh, my God!" With that appeal, his features faded into the column of blue and the column itself went back into the library. Suddenly the noises she had heard earlier began again, and rose in intensity to a crescendo of mayhem. Frightened now, nearly out of her wits, the woman heard herself shouting, "Stop it! Stop! I have too much to do! This is my house! *My* house! Get out!"

As suddenly as it began, the maelstrom ended. The woman, as the echoes from the other world faded, suddenly was overcome by a feeling of calm, of peace. It was as if an uneasy truce was declared between a handsome visitor from sometime in the distant past, and a headstrong woman of the present.

Afterwards, she relates, working late, she sometimes felt a presence, but never heard anything or felt the smothering blanket of cold she felt the night of the final confrontation.

But her youngest daughter would sometimes awaken in the middle of the night, crying. When the woman would go to see what was the matter, her child would complain that there was a man in her room watching her. Other times she would complain that the same man had come into her room and sat down on her bed.

She never said anything to her husband about what was happening late at night on the floor below where he slept. He was a skeptic and she was afraid he'd simply laugh at her and make fun. Apparently the sounds never travelled to the second floor: No one in the family ever mentioned any noises or was awakened by the cacophony in the library. But her story finally came out one morning after he came down for breakfast and asked her if she felt something—or someone—lay down on the bed between them that night.

Of course she had—and she probably had a pretty good idea of what the unseen sleeper looked like—and she proceeded to tell her husband of the handsome man who had once emerged from the recurring column of blue to scold her for using a space that, once in time, was evidently vitally important to him.

Townsmen Of A Stiller Town

They will come together again under higher bidding,
and will know their place and name.
This army will live, and live on,
so long as soul shall answer soul....

—Major General Joshua Chamberlain

A battlefield is many things to many people. To some who manage to visit Gettysburg only once or twice in their lives, it is a somewhat mysterious place where something monstrously horrible and important happened a very long time in the past. To others who have an opportunity to study the feats men accomplished here, it is a never-ending source of wonderment. To still others who spend vast amounts of their lives reading and re-reading about the battle, and great amounts of their money to visit and spend days on the field, it is truly a sacred place, truly a land hallowed by a great blood-letting: One gigantic national sacrificial alter for a whole segment of a generation of Americans.

But to those who fought at Gettysburg, it was either all of those things, or none of them. Those fortunate enough to survive the three-day holocaust found themselves, soul-drawn to return at reunion times and as often as their mortality would allow, until they too joined the ranks of their former comrades-in-arms, no longer strong, youthful soldiers but now, "townsmen of a stiller town."[1]

Most of those who died here, of course, probably only visited the place once, but that was enough. Or perhaps it wasn't.

The University Grays—Company A, 11th Mississippi Volunteers—were from the area around the college town of Oxford, Mississippi. Over half the company, when it was recruited in 1861, came directly from the classrooms of Ole Miss. Well-to-do, and intelligent, they could have been considered a cut above the common Confederate soldier, perhaps even officer material, had they wanted it that way. But most shunned the epaulets of command and put on the rough-cut frock coats of the rank and file infantryman. For most, once they got to Gettysburg, that common gray cloth would become their winding sheets.

Most Gettysburgians are at least vaguely aware of the carnage wrought by the two great armies literally outside their kitchen doors. Though they may live in warm, comfortable, modern homes, they realize that in another time not so long ago, the very space they now occupy in their rocker next to the fire was likely once occupied by a scurrying soldier—as in those houses, including my own, on the north end of town where the Union retreat took place. Or, where they lay their head to rest on their pillow upstairs was once in the flight path of a ten pounder Parrott shell. Or, as in some of the houses in the modern housing development called Colt Park right on the edge of the fields of Pickett's Charge, they cook their barbecues and play with their children very near where once a line of infantry—the University Grays, in fact—marched in ordered, doomed quickstep into a horizontal wall of minie balls and canister to their own immolation a few hundred feet hence. Of the seventy-nine who originally signed up with the Grays in 1861, only thirty-some were left to make the charge on that lurid last day at Gettysburg. Of those, fourteen were killed and seventeen were wounded. But numbers are not enough, are they? We can tell you the names of the gentle, bookish souls if you want: John Moore; Lieutenant Baker; Private De Gaffenreid; and the child Tom McKie, whose frantic mother wrote Confederate

President Jefferson Davis asking her son be spared, and whose fervent prayers for his safety were answered for ten battles, until Gettysburg. Some brutish clump of hot iron caught him full in the chest; Mrs. McKie need not pray any more.

Field of Pickett's Charge south of Colt Park.

Perhaps this all explains, in some disconnected way, why one woman, although an immaculate housekeeper, continues to smell at odd, random moments in her modern house in Colt Park, the horrid, sickly-sweet odor of rotting meat. A quick spray of air freshener and the smell is gone. But then, sometimes weeks or months later, unexpectedly, there is that whiff of rancid flesh floating in the same space—but at a different time—where it once, in reality, may have floated.

And while the ghostly, putrid odors may be explained away by some not necessarily understood mental process, what's harder to explain are the times her teenaged daughter would awaken in the middle of the night, suffocating, complaining of a choking feeling, as if unseen hands were twisting and clawing at her throat. It happened not once, to be tossed off as a bad dream, but many times, in that same space where men once clawed at their own throats for breath that would never come again.

You see, when the physical space is the same, sometimes it literally is only a matter of time.

The battlefield is also a place of recreation and escape for many who live here. Bicyclists, joggers, and evening walkers all enjoy their spare time on the avenues through the National Park. But whether they realize it or not, they are never very far from where men's mortal souls took that last long flight by the thousands into that eternal night.

A local man who, as a teenager, would seek solace late into the evening on the battlefield told of a couple of odd experiences, one at Spangler's Spring, the other on Little Round Top.

He related how, one evening as he rode his bicycle in toward Spangler's Spring from the Baltimore Road, just before he got to the area of the spring, he glanced off into the broad field to the left. Having lived in Gettysburg all his life, he was probably aware of the story that has recurred over the years of a tall, graceful figure—obviously a woman—moving ethereally through Pardee Field just over the hill from Spangler's Spring, moving, then bending down, then moving some more, as if searching, some say, for a fallen lover slain in the raw carnage of the fighting on Culp's Hill. He was also aware of those odd mists that seem to have been draped like a vast burial shroud in the evenings across many sections of the battlefield. Yet one night one of the wisps of fog caught his eye as being slightly out of place, a little too animated, a little too upright, as it moved about the open field near the spring once sought by thirsty, wounded soldiers for its life sustaining liquid.

He described it as a "glowing, phosphorescent specter," as he paused to watch as it moved from place to place about the field once filled with the helpless chaff of battle. Obviously too purposeful for any windborne fog, perhaps could it be some dear good Samaritan still compelled by truly overwhelming charity, to wander in search of those in need through all eternity?

Field near Spangler's Spring.

He also admits to running away from home one night, for whatever youthful reason he has now forgotten, and ending up on the western slope of Little Round Top late one evening, and inadvertently falling asleep there, in the warm misty magic of a summer's night in Gettysburg. He awakened some hours later with a start, realizing how long he had been there, well into the early morning hours. And as he began to rise to leave, his gaze was drawn to something strange happening in the valley below him.

Lights—not the twinkle of early evening fireflies but numerous stronger, glowing, yellowish lights—floated about

Plum Run valley just a hundred yards or so below, in seemingly random fashion. They would move, then he would see one stop, then move on, then another would stop, and move on, as if conducting some sort of search.

He seemed confused about what he saw and what it meant, until I mentioned to him that he wasn't the first to have seen that strange nocturnal display.

Others had seen that same sight in the same valley over the years. But all those sightings were merely repeats of the original scene enacted over a century and a quarter ago throughout the long night of July 2, 1863, when wounded soldiers witnessed the candles and oil lamps and lanterns of men searching the Valley of Death for comrades wounded in the day's fighting. Moving, then stopping to try to recognize a face twisted in death, then moving on, then stopping....

The look on his face can only be described as one of confused relief: Relief that he finally knew what those lights meant; confused because he knew with certainty that the heartfelt emotions of men searching for wounded comrades, just like the phantom lights after the passing of a long century, should have faded by now into the darkness.

And finally there is the recurring tale of the horseman. In one 48 hour period, I had no less than three people come to me and ask if I had heard any stories about a horseman on the field. One recounted the often told story of the ghostly equestrian who picks his way down the west slope of Little Round Top on certain mist-veiled nights, headless.[2]

There are countless stories of people hearing mounted men in column, passing by in the middle of the night, on some nocturnal ride through time in different areas in and near Gettysburg. I've forgotten how many people over the years have mentioned being awakened early in the first hours of the morning by horses trotting by when there were no horsemen to be seen. We know of the guests at the old Cashtown Inn who were awakened by horses impatiently pawing at the ground.[3] But at the other side of Adams county—once criss-crossed by horsemen of both Union and Confederate armies—there are stories of a young woman being awakened in the middle of the night by horses whinnying and pawing outside her bedroom window. She was truly frightened because this farmhouse was several miles from town and several hundred yards from her nearest neighbor. When she looked out to confront the trespassers who had ridden up on horseback, no one was to be seen. Of course the house is just off Low Dutch Road, one of the main routes back and forth as General George Armstrong Custer's Union cavalrymen cut across to engage Jeb Stuart's Confederate Cavalry at East Cavalry Battlefield.

The Wheatfield.

Someone recently mentioned seeing a man on horseback ride up to them in—of all places—the Wheatfield at dusk, dressed in the fine but dusty uniform of a Union officer. He tipped his hat, nodded and said hello as he rode by and excused himself for he had serious work before him, then turned his horse's head to ride back into what was once death's own playground. The visitors to the Wheatfield were pleased. Although they knew of no reenactment that weekend, it added to the ambience to see an authentically dressed officer and beautiful horse on the battlefield. Their smiles faded as they watched him ride a few more yards then vanish, taking with him a thousand secrets of the ages.

Finally, a member of the Gettysburg Police Department told me of his experience late one night in the early 1970s at the High Water Mark. Although some parts of the battlefield are officially closed to visitors after 10:00 P.M., local law enforcement officials would sometimes enter the battlefield roads on quiet nights so that they could be a stone's throw from their patrol duties and still be able to catch up on some paperwork. Settling down with a cup of coffee and his forms, this particular officer had parked at the famous "Angle" in the stone wall where Southern valor passed its most trying test. Pickett's Charge—or Longstreet's Assault, depending upon which historian you talk to—had punctured the Union line at that point. During the assault, by practical necessity, only a few Confederate officers were allowed to ride their mounts because of the perfect targets they would make. Those who did ride were shot down in the titian mist that rose from the fields in front of the stone wall.

The officer was deeply into his work before he paused for a minute to rest.

He looked up to see some sort of movement out in the darkened fields across the wall. As another minute passed he realized that it was a man in uniform on horseback, riding up to the wall only a dozen or so yards away.

The officer knew that the National Park Service had obtained horses the year before and was successfully using them for both historical interpretation and law enforcement. He even knew one of the rangers who rode, but couldn't tell as he waved to the late night equestrian, whether it was his acquaintance or not. As if oblivious to the officer's wave and even to the presence of a police patrol car, the mounted man continued to scan the once ghastly, darkened fields. The officer said the horse and rider stood for several minutes, then, still scanning the night, slowly he rode off into the darkness.

Later, the policeman confronted his ranger friend and asked him why he didn't acknowledge his presence when he was off on his midnight ride. Confusion crossed the ranger's face as he listened to the story. It wasn't he that took the horse out on a midnight ride. Nor, to his knowledge, was it any other ranger; the horses were on a full, strict, daytime riding schedule and, to his knowledge, needed their rest and were not allowed to be taken out on dangerous night-time rides by anyone.[4]

Incredulous, the Gettysburg police officer was left pondering what it was he had seen so distinctly across the wall once fought over by American Cains and Abels.

Fall Of The Sparrow

What has gone takes something with it,
and when this is of the dear, nothing can fill the place.
All the changes touched the borders of sorrows.

—Major General Joshua Chamberlain

Most experts agree that a "haunting" is the recurrence in the same venue of the same or similar paranormal happenings; when similar paranormal happenings occur to many different people over a number of years, a house or an area can truly be considered haunted.

Devil's Den must surely fall into this category. Old Dorm, Schmucker Hall at the Seminary, Stevens Hall, the houses on Baltimore Street and Carlisle Street, and a number of historic houses on and around the battlefield have had numerous inhabitants who have reported similar unexplainable sights and happenings. Iverson's Pits apparently at one time had a great deal of paranormal activity, which, at least in one case, has continued.

Prior to the massive expansion in recent years of Gettysburg College, two quaint houses stood across from the College Union Building and south of the Health Center, about where the new dining hall addition stands today.

They were two and a half stories high and were called, respectively, East Cottage and West Cottage, and housed female students for the most part. One was white stucco and stood until just a few years ago when it was razed. One must wonder where the displaced spirit went that was heard to wander in it by the numerous students who co-habitated with it.

No one would ever go into the attic of the cottage even though a good bit of storage space was there. It seems that virtually every time someone opened the small door in one of the second floor rooms that led up to the attic and attempted to climb the stairs, odd noises would begin—stifled moans, muffled voices, threatening sounds—until the intruder was driven to leave the area and close the door.

One woman, who lived there as a student, recalled the experiences that were had by her and the other residents of the house. At first they began blaming the personal items that were out-of-place on each other playing pranks. But strange things happened so often that even the most hard-core prankster would soon be expected to tire of them and admit to being the perpetrator—unless no *living* resident of the house was the cause of the happenings.

She thought the spirit must be classified as a "poltergeist" or "noisy ghost," because of the odd physical manifestations of its presence and the tireless repetitiveness of the events. The poet Robert Graves, writing about "noisy ghosts" in 1958 said that "poltergeists everywhere show an appalling sameness of behavior; humorless, pointless, uncoordinated." Poltergeists have run amok in nearly every country, and for quite a while too: one of the first cases was recorded in Germany in A. D. 355.[1] Yet, how many unexplainable occurrences of physical objects—stone implements or animal skin clothing or pottery—being moved happened before that date and were never recorded or even spoken of, the percipient fearful of an angry god or evil spirit?

The women in East Cottage would, one by one, clean up, make their beds and leave for morning classes. They would study after class in the library, or be busy until noon, when they would all manage to return to the cottage to have lunch. Sure enough, one of the beds would be torn up and disheveled, pillows here, covers there. One of the housemates would get the blame and profess her innocence, until it had happened enough times to everyone in the house that some other presence was eventually blamed.

East Cottage (Special Collections, Gettysburg College Library).

The woman who related this story later worked for the National Park Service and had some further experiences out on the battlefield, some of which are recorded in this book. But none was quite as disconcerting as those she experienced in East Cottage.

Her room was on the second floor. She had a bookshelf in that room that had a raised edge—a "lip"—at the front of the shelf to keep the books from tumbling. A half-dozen books were lying upon the shelf on their sides—not upright as they normally are—and she watched one night in utter amazement as one by one each book lifted over the lip and fell to the floor.

She and the other women were the victims several times of the messy poltergeist when it threw papers around individual rooms while they were gone.

They would sometimes be awakened late at night by the old piano downstairs playing by itself. No specific tune, just a random tinkling of keys. At first they thought it was a mouse or squirrel, but never could confirm the unlikely event that some timid creature like that would wander up and down the keys of a noisy piano without scaring itself. There were never any other normal signs of rodent infestation—chewed windows, food nibbled at, droppings—to confirm the fact that it was a living creature and not a spiritual one who was attracted time and again to the half-century-old instrument to play some mournful, ethereal music on the keys.

Perhaps the time that the poltergeist evoked the most anger was when my friend's small, porcelain, Hummel-type music box with a figurine was flipped off the bookshelf onto the floor to smash into several pieces. It was the same bookshelf with the lipped edge on it, from which books would unexplainably tumble. Disappointment gave way to confusion as to how the heavy figurine could have lifted itself from the shelf, over the lip, and hurled itself to the floor without the least bit of movement within the house or movement of the shelf itself or anything else on it. In fact, it would have taken an earthquake to lift the weighted music box over the edge of the shelf and toss it carelessly to the floor. And of course, no earthquakes have been recorded in Gettysburg in the last century-and-a-half, unless you want to count the unleashing of hundreds of cannon in three horrid days in July 1863. Her anger came later, as she was trying to carefully glue the pieces back together since the figurine held much sentimental value. "All right," she scolded angrily into thin air when a piece would not stick. "I've had it with you! That's enough!" For a long time there was no more activity in the house.

Then, one day, she was standing in the kitchen of the cottage. The door to the unfinished cellar was closed and locked with its skeleton key. The old door was apparently out of joint and the women noticed that if they didn't lock the ancient lock with the key, they would find the door open in the mornings. They never used the basement for anything, but stored canned goods in the stairway.

Suddenly, her attention was attracted by some movements at the door. As she watched, the key in the old door slowly turned by itself, the door came unlocked and swung open as if letting someone out of the kitchen and down into the darkened cellar.

As if something was trying to say that it was sorry for breaking the figurine and was banishing itself from the house, it was the last thing, to her knowledge, that ever happened in the cottage.

*   *   *

Eventually the cottages were torn down and the new dining hall addition was constructed. Just fifty yards or so from where East and West Cottages once stood is the Health Center for the college. From the Health Center you can look out across West Broadway, across the broad, grassy athletic fields where now rich boys play and once brave boys died, to the ridgeline of Oak Ridge, from which streamed the destroyed remnants of a portion of the Union Army's First Corps. You must also remember that the 47 barren acres between Oak Ridge, Broadway, Howard Avenue, and the Carlisle Road were irreverently and irreversibly altered by Gettysburg College in the last few years, filling in with thousands of truckloads of fill the valleys and small defilades which saved soldier's lives, for their fields of play. "Hallowed ground" means different things to different people.

Somewhere in those fields between the ridgeline and the college retreated what was left of the 11th Pennsylvania, losing sight of their little mascot in the confusion. Their small war dog "Sallie" got lost in the melee then stayed behind to guard her fallen masters. Guard them she did with the unconditional, selfless, mysterious love given only by dogs, going without food or water for three stifling days, ferociously keeping Confederates—or anyone—away from the bodies of the dead Pennsylvanians until the survivors of the 11th returned to bury their brother soldiers. Then and only then, when she recognized her comrades would the brave little terrier yield the high ground of Oak Ridge and allow the bodies of her slain masters to be touched. Yes, "hallowed ground" is understood differently by different creatures.

Across the fields tumbled the men from Pennsylvania and Massachusetts, New York and Maine. They retreated into the town along the railroad bed to the west and the Mummasburg Road, with ragged edges of their retreating lines making their way through the crop-filled fields. If they could have looked into the future (or we into the past) they would have been seen passing through the brick walls of the modern building of the Health Center.

Time is such a mysterious thing. The different ways we measure it, loosely based upon the turning of the earth relative to the sun, or even with atomic clocks, seem inadequate toward understanding time's true nature. There is the time which flows forward and is measured by pieces on our wrists or on the walls or in towers and keeps us coordinated with the rest of the world. More important is the time ticked off by our own bodies that represents the gradual decay of our physical forms, because when that clock stops, so do we. The only real reason time matters is death, and so we must be very careful with the way we kill time before it eventually kills us.

But what happens to time when we die?

Some parapsychologists believe that the sightings of apparitions indicate life after death, that the dead person is the one sending the telepathic message to the living.[2] And if we do indeed move on, into another form or world, certainly some form of time must occur, because in order to exist in any form, something must be in existence for at least some time. Some philosophers have called it universal time, or even God's Time, wherein time travels not forward—in fact, doesn't even flow—but merely exists as "now." The existence somewhere of an ageless, timeless, non-decaying, "now" certainly explains the immutability and eternal nature of those gone before us.

One of the nurses who worked the night shift at the Health Center in the mid-1980s recalled some experiences she had—as well as others—in the center established for the healing of students.

Alone in the semi-darkened Health Center at night, she would often hear footfalls coming down the hall toward the nurse's office. She would leave her desk to try and help whatever student had gotten up to wander the halls, but no one was there. The only times that the sounds of the footsteps up and down the halls were frightening were when she knew that no one was checked into the center that night. Those times she called College Security, who came promptly and found no one to arrest.

There were odd noises as well. For some of noises she could locate the source: photos falling off the wall; radiator covers being flung from the radiators. Yet, even though she could locate where the noise came from, she was still anxious about just how frequently the photos would fall. How many times in a week or two do several different radiator covers have to end up crashing to the floor before one suspects something odd: eight, ten times? How often should a picture fall, the nail inspected, the picture re-hung only to fall again, before one is convinced that someone unseen is trying to do a little re-decorating: six times, eight times?

Finally, when the odd noises continued one night as she was catching up on backlogged paperwork to the soft background buzz of the television, they became so loud and irritating, she simply accepted the cacophony and turned up the volume of the TV to cover the noises so she wouldn't be distracted from her work.

She said that her evenings there alone were usually filled with the constant feeling that someone else was around. Her sense, which may be colored by her devotion to her profession, was that whoever was walking the halls was not malevolent, but merely checking in on the sick students, whether there were any in the building or not. And yet, even with knowing the kindly nature of the invisible, caring spirit who paces and re-arranges things, she admits to being much happier about not working nights anymore.

Death's Feast

These were my men,
and those who followed were familiar and dear.
They belonged to me and I to them,
by bonds birth cannot create nor death sever.
More were passing here than the personages on the
stand could see.
But to me so seeing, what a review,
how great, how far, how near!
It was as the morning of the resurrection!

—Major General Joshua Chamberlain

There is always a momentary pause upon confronting a great anachronism that looms before our senses occasionally in life. The tangle of thoughts when we discover that someone we love and just saw alive is suddenly dead; the image that rises, in some strange way, upon being hurt or wounded, that the person I have known all my life—"me"—might be in danger of dying at this moment; the mistrust of the senses before any of us is willing to surrender what we believe is true to what is reality. Yet, when you have lived in one of the historic houses on the battlefield of Gettysburg, the occasional suspension of reality is acceptable. So it was with two of my friends who lived in houses that rest upon the hallowed ground of Gettysburg.

I received a letter from a good friend now living in Washington who, for a time, worked for the National Park Service at Gettysburg and lived in at least one of the historic houses on the battlefield. She told me of two events in the letter of which I was unaware.

First, she mentioned a mutual friend who was living in the George Weikert House; the same Weikert House that contained the upstairs door that refused to remain closed no matter what anyone did to it, including nailing it shut.[1] Her roommate travelled frequently in her job for the National Park Service and she was alone in the house watching television one night. The drone of the TV had gone on for a while, when she was suddenly aware of another noise in the house besides the TV—what some acoustics experts might call "white noise"—a sort of underlying, background noise which is so monotonous in pitch that it is hardly even noticeable without paying strict attention to it. She got up and walked to the TV and turned down the volume. The sounds became more distinct now, and she heard the unmistakable murmur of what she called a "party" going on somewhere within the confines of the house. People were chattering, glasses clinking, movement of bodies. She distinctly heard it on the second floor of the house.

The Weikert House.

The sounds of the party went on as she became more and more aware. Laughter, faint music, doors opening and closing, glasses with ice tinkling quietly above her head.

She turned up the TV volume again, wandered back to the sofa with a slight smile growing on her face, knowing exactly what was happening but still unwilling to surrender all of reason to the unreasonable. Again she rose and turned down the volume, and again listened to the polite hum of her uninvited guests upstairs.

Finally, gaining enough courage from the fact that this, indeed, was her house, she began to ascend the stairs as the festivities continued and she listened, a reluctant party-crasher. As she approached the second floor, the sounds slowly began to fade, as if a heavy, dark curtain were pulled across the entranceway to another era. By the time she reached the second floor, all the sounds had ceased.

A few weeks later she was sitting with her roommate who had returned from her trip and casually, and somewhat reluctantly, mentioned the strange party noises that stirred her to try to join the festivities on the second floor of their home: the laughing, the glasses clinking, the sounds of low voices, the music. Related to her roommate, it was almost as if she were trying to elicit the comforting response of "how strange…maybe you were dreaming...couldn't have happened."

Instead, her roommate listened, smiled and said, "Oh. You heard it too," and told of the number of times she had heard the ghostly revelry on the second floor of Mr. Weikert's old stone house.

Further on in the letter, my friend from Washington described a quiet evening at home she and her new husband were having, relaxing in the brick structure they rented we all called "The Schoolhouse," which sits on the northeast slope of Little Round Top. It probably wasn't there at the time of the battle, but is very old, and actually had been, at one time, a one room schoolhouse. It retains much of the ambience of a little red schoolhouse and, if the interior had not been remodeled, upon approaching the house you would swear that when you opened the door you would be greeted by the murmur of children learning their lessons out loud in the old style "blab-school" fashion, and be met by the icy gaze of a stern, tight-laced "school-marm."

As she and her husband sat there that particular night, slowly, almost imperceptibly at first, her antique rocker began to rock back and forth. Gradually, the rocking motion grew as she and her husband watched. She looked at him, then at the windows to see if perhaps a breeze had moved it. But all the windows were closed, and the rocking continued. Slowly, just as it had started, the rocker gradually swung to a halt.

The Little Red Schoolhouse.

It was almost as if the spirit of one of the teachers long gone had returned to the beloved old one-room schoolhouse, one more time, to teach one last lesson about life and what appears to be death....

* * *

We return to the area of Iverson's Pits, that one spot on the battlefield where over 500 North Carolina soldier-boys were sent on the last long march toward eternity at virtually the same moment by thousands of Yankee minie balls, and were buried where they dropped in a common grave a furlong wide.[2]

The story comes again from one of Dr. Charles Emmons's students who had done a paper on supernatural occurrences on the battlefield.[3] A student from Gettysburg College had taken his girlfriend from another college out on the battlefield around midnight. The Peace Light Memorial and its parking area are a short drive from the Gettysburg College Campus, and the light from the monument provides a romantic setting. An observation tower on Oak Ridge is located nearby and is another popular spot from which to view the town at night.

The young woman was described as being "quite psychic," one of those individuals tuned in, so to speak, to the quiet, unseen stirrings in the other world. She had seen, one night, an old woman appear in her apartment and walk into her closet only to vanish amongst the clothing stored there. Later she learned that indeed, an elderly woman had entered that closet decades before, but left it only as a corpse separated from its departed spirit. She died by hanging herself in that very closet the young woman once watched her enter, but never leave.

It was a foggy night. They had left the car and were sitting near the small tower, by one of the stone fences that once sheltered Union infantry from Confederate gunfire, near where the battlefield road from the Peace Light crosses the Mummasburg Road. It was from that site where the Union line was "refused"—doubled back upon itself in the direction of the town—and from where their musketry delivered virtually a solid wall of lead to the west: Hundreds of minie balls launched within a tenth of a second of one another, against the men of Iverson's Brigade. Confederates just eighty or so yards from the wall by the hundreds felt the electric shock to the nervous system, the total disruption of senses an intrusion upon the body like that produces. The lucky ones died instantly, struck in the head or the heart. The unlucky ones fell writhing, only to be wounded again and again. All, no doubt in their last moments, after being caught in the open, desperately thought of rising and trying to make it to cover. None did, except in his final, dying dreams.

The young man was looking out towards the northern end of Gettysburg and she towards the Peace Light. Suddenly, her eye was caught by a rapid motion in the misty dark fields not more than a few dozen feet from where she sat. Her breath caught in her throat as she realized it was a "grayish figure," carrying a rifle and running quickly through the field just beyond the low stone wall. Whoever it was appeared to take cover behind two trees. Though close enough to see both her and her boyfriend, the misty figure was more intent upon finding shelter than making contact with anyone. She quickly grabbed the arm of her boyfriend and hurried back to the parked car.

She refused to tell him why she was in such a hurry to leave the place until they were safely within the car. As they drove out of the parking lot, the car headlights illuminated the two trees, and both passengers peered into the mist to see if the strange figure was to be seen behind the foliage. He was apparently well hidden, for they saw no sign of him behind the twin trees.

Later she was to describe the figure as "real"—meaning humanlike—appearing "unfocused," lit only by the flickering, uncertain light from the Peace Light. Its sudden appearance and lack of interest in the two other people just yards away sent a queasy feeling through her stomach.

The morning after she had seen the image dart behind the two trees in the fog, they drove out to the tower again to examine the site in broad daylight. As they parked the car and re-created the night-scene which occurred just hours before, they were shocked by one unexplainable fact: There were no longer two trees which they so clearly saw the night before, but only one. As they approached the single tree they realized that right next to it was the stump of another. But instead of being freshly cut, it was gnarled and rotted and weathered, obviously the work of some woodsman of decades before, now himself probably long dead.

Tree and stump near Iverson's Pits.

Like Iverson's Burial Pits, where the poor souls whose last wish for a few horrifying minutes on July 1,1863, was to find shelter from the burning lead being fired at them, the protection they coveted with the last of their life's blood also had disappeared....

They say there are no atheists in foxholes. There can be no doubt that the experience of combat, the unreal-ness of the scene surrounding a soldier when watching close friends pass from animation to something else either causes him to abandon completely any faith he may have had, or believe more deeply in an afterlife. Shakespeare's admonition that "there are few die well that die in a battle," is no doubt true: Soldiers, before they have reached a certain fatalistic stage while facing combat think back on all the things they will miss; on their wives and sweethearts and parents and children; on the worldly possessions they may be leaving behind; on home. But soon the fatalism takes over, the realization—or the coping device—that makes them believe that if their time is up, it is up; that there is a bullet out there with their name on it, so don't worry about all the other bullets flying by.

Perhaps it is then that the concept of an afterlife crosses the soldier's mind, as it has for untold centuries. Paradise. Heaven. The Happy Hunting Ground. Valhalla. The place where warriors go when they die if they've done their duty.

The belief that he and his loved ones will meet again permeates many soldiers' letters and diaries, and though they may have never had any organized religion in their lives, they seem to understand and accept the concept and hope for some sort of afterlife, perhaps because they realize they will leave something behind, something quite unfinished....

In the past several years a number of America's finest artists have turned to recreating the past in their paintings. Following "in the brush strokes" of military artists like Frederick Remington, Eduoard DeTaille, and some contemporary masters like Tom Lea and Tom Lovett, they have chosen to represent men at war. Since no photos were ever taken of a Civil War battle, we must rely upon an artist to show us the look on the men's faces as they moved into combat, the posture of their bodies, the fear in their eyes. From this we learn even more of the awful details of the American Civil War.

Most of the artists painting today are fine researchers as well. Since a soldier's kepi sometimes fell top-down on the battlefield, they must know what the inside looked like. Since Shiloh doesn't look like Gettysburg, and Antietam doesn't look like Stone's River, the artists visit the sites where the battles took place.

One of the finest of these artists now painting was researching here in Gettysburg and staying with his wife in a modern motel just on the edge of the battlefield. In fact, his room was located only a couple of hundred yards from where Pickett's Charge passed to find itself wasted on the gentle, fire-ringed slopes of Cemetery Ridge. Some of the Northern soldiers who died defending the Union line were buried even closer to where he and his wife slept that night, in the National Cemetery just a hundred or so yards away, enjoying sleep's viler sister, death.

It was about two in the morning when the artist started to hear it. A soft movement of what initially sounded like some of the jewelry he and his wife left on the dresser as they prepared for bed. At first he was a little disgusted to think that a fine modern motel like the one they had rented had mice. His wife was awakened by the rattling as well and quietly mentioned it to him. Slowly, silently he raised himself from the bed and flipped on the light to catch the little critters in the act and call the night desk clerk to report them.

No rodent was on the desk. The jewelry appeared to be in the same place where his wife had left it. Nothing appeared to have been moved. He went over to the window to see if anyone was out in the parking lot trying to break into their car. But it was the off-season in Gettysburg and there was only one other car in the lot, and no one was near it. Perplexed, but not hearing the noises anymore, he turned the light back out and reclined. Apparently, whatever it was, it was gone.

Then it started again. This time it came from a corner of the room. In a recent conversation, asked what it sounded like, he said that, more than anything it was like the chain of an old-fashioned pocket watch being rattled. Again the lights were flipped on and their attention concentrated on the corner from where the odd rattling emanated. Again, there was no mouse, or watch chain, or anything else to visually confirm the strange sounds they both heard.

Out went the lights again. It was quiet in the darkened room. Both were about to fall off to sleep, when again the rattling began, this time across the room from where they'd heard it before. Again, the lights were turned on, but nothing was seen.

Modern Steinwehr Avenue and motels.

For another hour the unexplainable jingling that sounded like a pocket watch being handled went on, first on this side of the room, then on that side of the room in the motel that was built on the one corner of earth where a great nation's destiny was decided and its beloved boys were hideously harvested for death's abundant feast.

Though it wasn't the most restful night they ever spent, they finally got some sleep. Yet one must wonder what could have happened on that very spot during the fire and fury of battle that was so important that it demanded continual attention to the hands of the watch; and who could it have been that was so concerned with temporal time as to keep removing a pocket watch and replacing it over and over; and why would the sound so much associated with timekeeping in the 19th Century continue in this particular space through almost thirteen decades?

Pirouettes In Quicksand

There are things belonging to the eternities
of which you've but lately heard:
Things of the past;
things of the present;
things yet to be.
Oh, break these worldly wings so I may finally fly...

—Anonymous

Probably the best-known psychic in this area is Karyol
Kirkpatrick of Lancaster. I first met her when we both visited
two Gettysburg "haunted houses" on Halloween morning in
1991 for a live broadcast for a local radio station.

While she has helped several police departments solve
murders that had them stumped by finding incriminating
hidden evidence psychically, she doesn't like to mention who
the murderers are or where they are incarcerated. As it was
explained to me by a mutual friend, many murderers are
themselves psychic, but use their remarkable powers to tap
into the evil energies which co-exist along side of the good.

Her amazing observations in the Gettysburg "haunted
houses" are chronicled in this book. My experience with her
was so interesting that I asked her if she would like to visit
some areas on the Gettysburg Battlefield to see what she
could pick up from them. Her one and only trip to Gettysburg
had been when she visited the two houses on Halloween. She
had never been out on the battlefield before in her life—or
at least, in this life. Needless to say we were both looking
forward to the visit.

On July 27, 1992, she had a radio broadcast to do in Hanover, so we met afterwards for breakfast and then drove to Gettysburg with her "designated driver," Dorothea Fasig and Dorothea's son Mike. (Karyol never drives. When engaged in psychic activity, she sometimes lapses into a trance and is fearful that it could happen sometime when she is driving.) Jeane Thomas was our chauffeur around the battlefield.

Because of temperament and training, I've always felt as if I've been on the fringe of many things in life; it is the proper place for a writer to exist. I'm close enough to experience life, but far enough removed to write about it, if not objectively, then certainly with a universality. So when I say I approached my battlefield experience with Karyol as a skeptic, I don't mean it in a pejorative sense. I have approached all the ghost stories in this book and the last with the same healthy skepticism, which is actually more of a "show me and I'll believe you" attitude than denial.

The Triangular Field.

So our first stop was the Triangular Field where so many cameramen (and camerawomen) have had such bad luck with their equipment.[1]

What is now known as the Triangular Field was once owned by Mr. George W. Weikert, and was a field separate from the fields surrounding Weikert's farmhouse located about 1000 feet to the west and rented by the Timbers family. The Triangular Field held a bloody past born within a few dreadful hours on a hot July day for Georgians and Texans, New Yorkers and Pennsylvanians.

On the afternoon of July 2,1863, the men of General James Longstreet's Confederate Corps—specifically Major General John Bell Hood's Division—were launched in an assault from their positions on the southern end of Seminary Ridge toward the left flank of the Union line near a large, wooded hill called Round Top. As the four lines of infantry descended the slope of southern Seminary Ridge and entered the valley of the small creek called Rose Run, they were perfect targets for artillery fire from the four cannon of Smith's 4th New York Battery. After two years of drill and battle, Smith's New Yorkers were excellent artillerists. They were cutting fuses for five and six seconds in an attempt to explode the projectiles over the heads of the Southerners, showering them with hot, jagged pieces of iron. The men of the 1st Texas Regiment along with the 3rd Arkansas continued to advance courageously down the slope as Smith's men ran out of case shot and shell and changed to canister.

Man's creativity is never so twisted nor as inventive as when it is engaged in finding new ways to kill in battle. Canister consisted of what was virtually a tin can filled with scores of lead or iron balls. Though the range was short, when the gun was fired the tin can disintegrated and the balls spewed out in a horrifying hail of pain and death. One eyewitness recalled that the change in ammunition tore "gap after gap through the ranks of the advancing foe."[2] That's a nice way of saying that human beings were literally blown apart by the force of the impact of several canister balls in a relatively small area on the body.

The 3rd Arkansas had their left flank turned and thus were forced to retire and leave the Texans to their own fate. The Texans alone charged Smith's battery but were driven back by canister from the battery and an impetuous charge by the 124th New York led by Major Cromwell. Just as they victoriously drove the Texans down the slope of the Triangular Field, down went Cromwell tumbling backward out of the saddle, a southern minie ball through his heart. Along with the major, the volley from the recently arrived 15th Georgia knocked down nearly a quarter of the Orange Blossoms. Orange County, New York's beloved sons were being torn to pieces in that three-sided cinerary. Yet another casualty in the seething hell was Colonel Ellis of the 124th. Lifting his sword to give a command that would only be heard echoing in another world, he took rebel lead through his forehead and fell a tangled heap of quivering flesh amongst the stained rocks and sickening crimson harvest of this day's work in Mr. Weikert's field.

Nor was it over in the odd, three-cornered field. Georgians of General Benning's Brigade would try three more times to assault the slope of the weird field and be met by the hot, horrid breath of musketry from the 99th Pennsylvania as well as artillery fire from Little Round Top. A participant described it:

The conflict at this point defied description. Roaring cannon, crashing rifles, screeching shots, bursting shells, hissing bullets, cheers, shouts, shrieks and groans were the notes of the song of death which greeted the grim reaper, as with mighty sweeps he leveled down the richest field of grain ever garnered on this continent.[3]

And so it is that in human combat on the glorious field of battle, man's (and now soon woman's) mortal experience is reduced to the basest of all primary elements, and those reduced even further: earth, fire, water, air, rock, blood, dust, smoke, life, death.

Karyol Kirkpatrick took my tape recorder to the top edge of the Triangular Field and began recording her feelings. She entered a mental state where all her energy is focused upon what she feels from her surroundings, from the trees, the earth, the grass, the rocks. Our group was nowhere near her for about ten minutes while she spoke into the recorder. Those familiar with earlier stories of the Triangular Field will have no problem understanding that when Karyol returned with the modern machine, though she was familiar with that type of recorder, it had failed to work while she was anywhere near the field.

I fiddled with the machine, got it running again, and, from a safe distance away on the road, Karyol began recording her impressions again.

Some excerpts, verbatim, from the tape: "A lot of conflict and confusion as to what was going on. I felt as though...there was something of a sheltered area that I could hear like lots of hollering and crying out. I felt as though there were some people bound and I felt as though there were some people injured...It showed as though that there was...I could feel a man having his leg blown off right about the knee coming up the hill...." And more of the same.

She said she felt two feelings coming together here, as she pointed to the northwest corner of the field: A crying of victory and a crying of loss. To her, the momentum was the same for the two feelings, meaning that nobody had won and nobody had lost; the loss of life had been the greatest sacrifice.

The feeling I got from the overall was as though the trees could not absorb the spiritual energies and the fires and the weepings of the spirits, and it's like there wasn't enough angelic force to guide the spirits and souls and the weepings and the cryings as they were trying to leave their bodies. I felt as though much death and much blood to this area to this comer, [pointing again to the uppermost comer where the Texans charged and were driven back by the New Yorkers and later the Georgians charged] but I felt that it started over there and came this way [indicating the far bottom comer and lower wall of the field] as you come more this way it seemed as though that there were greater horrors that went on into and through the night.

Listening to the tape again, I realized that she was describing in non-historian terms, in general what went on in that once horrid field. The 1st Texas, combined with the 15th Georgia and the 20th Georgia, made their assault from the wall (now a remnant) at the bottom of the Triangular Field up the hill to the wall at the top of the field where Smith's Battery and the 99th Pennsylvania waited for them. The Georgia and Texas regiments straddled the wall and so were funneled right to the upper comer. The 20th hit the upper wall a little obliquely, and they, too, sidled a little to their left, toward the corner where Karyol was certain there was "much death and much blood."

For a non-historian who had never read anything about the battle other than who won, and who was visiting a rather out-of-the-way battlesite, she picked up something from the field itself which helped her describe the movements of troops across the battlesite very accurately. But that was nothing compared to what she said next.

She paused on the tape, seemingly exhausting what she could get from the area. She asked if I had picked up any key phrase in what she said and I replied that I would need to review the tape. I asked her if she wanted to know what happened here and she replied, "No, it doesn't matter." Precisely. Thanks to her gift she had just "seen" what had happened there; why would she need an historian to tell her!

She talked about a traitor and someone named Johnny being hanged, which didn't make any historical sense to me, at least as far as *my* knowledge of the battle-related history of the area was concerned. She also mentioned that she felt there were animals, water and the smell of food as she gestured toward the area of Rose Run and the Confederate main battle lines.

She continued: "There were animals deeper in here and there was some type of a shelter, a hospital and there were also people tied that they didn't want to get away and didn't want them to get hurt either." Again listening to the tape afterwards, I remember that the Timbers Farm once stood over in the direction Karyol pointed, and was, no doubt, used as a temporary hospital where men were taken. The tying up of people could possibly be a description of the men with head wounds who could still walk but had lost their very essences to the sloppy work of an ounce of flattened lead. What awful things a hot .58 caliber minie ball does once it is let loose inside a human skull to do its hideous dance.

She spoke again about that once horrifying corner, and that she felt that the trees were actually weeping because there was more than they could absorb.

She pointed to one of the larger rocks and said she felt a conversation between two people over the games that men play and the power over one another as well as the power to succeed. All it brought was death.

A few more comments and she wondered why the monuments were in one place and not another where she felt they should be. She was dead right about that. Historians at the park think that Smith's Battery now rests several yards behind where it may have been during the battle—at the wall. As well, the monument to the Orange Blossoms is at the top of the crest and not down in the oddly-shaped field where they paid so dearly for their moment of glory.

Another pause in the tape, and I asked a wild question of the woman who had never studied the battle and had never been on the site before: "Do you get any names of states, or anything?"

A long pause, then: "I wanted to say clay; Georgia clay." Another pause. "And they're not used to the brown earth...."

Some more about traveling on water and communications, and another pause.

Then: "I question even if there could have been some people out of or from close around Texas come through this area or region or was a part of this in some way or some manner."

A very long pause: "I wanted to feel that there were also people out of Philadelphia and maybe southern New York area and region here because they had a different accent." A short pause: "I can hear their voices...."

By now in awe, I asked her to record it on the tape to affirm that this was her first visit to this area. She confirmed that except for her visit to the two haunted houses within the town in October, this was, indeed, her only visit to the battlefield. She also added that she has only been interested in ancient history and not American History.

It was at that point I told her that the name of this area was the Triangular Field and that Benning's Georgians and the 1st Texas attacked and were driven back. I said at that point I didn't know about Philadelphia, but the troops that fought them initially were members of the 124th New York and pointed to the monument. I asked her if she had seen the monument before. (I was certain that she hadn't even looked in that direction, but I had to be sure.) She said no, she didn't even have her glasses on, which she would need to see anything that far away.

Looking at a map later, I discovered that Orange County is indeed in southern New York, along the New Jersey border.

Walking back to the van I looked up and saw the monument to the 99th Pennsylvania. Jeane asked Mike, the youngest of us, to run up to the monument and see where they were recruited.

"Philadelphia," he called down.

Our visit to the Wheatfield revealed that psychic time doesn't necessarily follow the same pattern of flow that real time does. Our visit to the battlefield reminded me of a visit to a hall with many windows and doors. Some of the doors were open and some of them shut; some of the windows were clear or open and some were closed or fogged over. You could not always pick which part of the great past you would be able to see.

In the Wheatfield, despite the incredible tumult which occurred there on July 2, 1863, Karyol had tapped into an earlier period. Mostly, she felt Native American spirits on that spot, standing, in fact, on one spot, she thought one important warrior had died. (Historians know only by oral accounts of a great Indian battle which occurred on the site where late-coming combatants would later shed their blood. Accounts place it somewhere in the vicinity of Big Round Top, perhaps to the south or west of it, close to where we were standing.) She also felt a lot of female energy in the area, nurses perhaps, helping with casualties, seeking to help the wounded from either era.

She did hear the clashing of metal, wood, and sticks and a great deal of hollering, but much of what she picked up was from several eras and somewhat disjointed. There are more stories to our ancient earth than we can ever know.

We began to move on to our next site. We drove along West Confederate Avenue toward the first day's battle site and, in particular, Reynolds Woods.

Major General John F. Reynolds was a native of Lancaster, Pennsylvania and had arrived upon the battlefield of Gettysburg just as it was becoming a battlefield, in the morning of July 1,1863. He was here barely long enough to make sure his Union Army First Corps was headed in the right direction as he sat his horse upon McPherson Ridge, when a rebel marksman sent a minie ball smashing into the back of his neck.

His aides thought first that he had just been stunned since they rolled him over and could find no wound except a bruise over his left eye. Then they realized he wasn't coming to and began to carry him back to the town. Halfway between the place where he was hit and the Seminary, Reynolds gasped a little. His aides paused with their burden and tried to give him some water, but he was insensible. When they got back to town and placed him in Mr. George's stone house on the pike to Emmitsburg, they saw where he had been hit, saw that there was very little blood, and assumed that the wound had bled internally.[4] From being offered the command of the largest army on the planet—The Union Army of the Potomac—just a week before, he instead became the highest-ranking officer from either side to die in the battle.

We had just passed the lovely McMillan House on the north end of West Confederate Avenue when Karyol said that she felt something was happening at the beginning. I had a moment of confusion until I realized that we were heading out to where the battle indeed had begun. Then she said something even more confusing when she said she felt a pain in her back.

The tape recorder wasn't going at that moment because we weren't near the site yet. As the van travelled out the Fairfield Road toward Doubleday Avenue, I turned and wondered if she was really in discomfort. She said something to the effect that, "I feel like someone was shot in the back. I feel the pain in my back."

We turned onto Doubleday Avenue and she said, "It's really getting stronger. I can feel the pain in my back." I noticed that she was actually sitting up, moving her back away from the seat and reaching behind her. Then I realized that she was relating to Reynolds somehow.

We pulled over at the site of the monument to Reynolds on the spot where he was struck. The monument is so far off the road that one would need to know exactly what one was looking for to find it, as well as very good eyesight to read it. I told her that we didn't even have to get out of the van for this one. I told her the story about Reynolds, ending with the details of his wounding in the back of the neck.

Reynolds Woods.

The suddenness of Karyol's pain and the growing intensity as we approached the site where Reynolds was struck in an anatomical area which probably produced an immediate, if only momentary shock of pain down his back truly impressed me and the others in the van. As far as an explanation for this remarkable woman's physical manifestations of empathy for an officer of an army long dead and gone, I have none.

Somewhere Between Worlds

When that this body did contain a spirit,
A kingdom for it was too small a bound...

—William Shakespeare,
King Henry IV, Act V, scene iv.

At Gettysburg, in the fields and valleys, on the ridges and from the rocks—wherever you go when it's quiet—you can almost hear the great breathing of history, barely audible, like a dull, continuous, rumble coming from the very earth below your feet.

No one is immune to the vortex that pulls us to the place; the high-born and lowly, the common visitor and the diplomat, the mere private soldier and the great general. The whole world comes to Gettysburg, eventually.

And so it was with Dwight David Eisenhower. The common Texas farm boy, who left the turning of the earth to lead great armies and defeat great evil that threatened to girdle the entire globe in chains, eventually came back to the farm. He had heard the rumblings of history at Gettysburg before he himself had made it, and returned, as great a man as he was, to be near an even greater place.

If the American Civil War was the great moral crusade of the 19th century, then World War II was the great moral crusade of the 20th. The main issue was virtually the same: Slavery. And while slavery as it was known in the antebellum American South had endured long enough to be a geographically restricted, regionally accepted institution, it was still enslavement. What the Nazis and Japanese warlords did, and what they intended to do with the rest of the world had no restrictions. As well as enslavement, it was what could have become annihilation.

Some men saw in the rantings of Hitler and the gobbling up of the Pacific Basin by the Japanese, a terror unknown to humankind on a stage of epic scale.

One of those men was Dwight Eisenhower, and when his time for ultimate effort and hard decisions came, he responded.

He had been to Gettysburg before—in his mind at least—as he studied the maps and texts as part of his military science courses at the U. S. Military Academy. After his graduation in 1915, instead of being sent to Europe during World War I, he was stationed at Gettysburg's Camp Colt, the training center for the U. S. Army's newly conceived tank corps.

The camp was situated in the middle of the fields once drenched by the rain of human blood during Pickett's Charge. Even though the youthful officer and his lovely young wife Mamie lived in two homes at separate times in the small town of Gettysburg, the man they called "Ike" had time to spend on the battlefield and learned its lessons well.

The bucolic fields, the small-town ambience, the friendliness of the people, and the great pull of history kept hold on their hearts for the rest of their lives. Over the next three decades they would travel extensively. After his service in World War II as Supreme Commander of Allied Forces in the invasion of Europe and a stint as president of Columbia University, Eisenhower and Mamie began looking for a place in which to retire. Not surprisingly, the soldier turned to a battlefield to find peace. Recalling their happy younger days in Gettysburg they purchased a small dairy farm in 1950. It was located in the rear of the Confederate lines, not far from where Major General Longstreet had his headquarters and within eyeshot of where Pickett's men mustered for their fateful summer's charge some 87 years before.

But easy retirement was not forthcoming. Eisenhower, very much like famous military commander General Robert E. Lee before him, for the first fifty years of his existence had lived his professional life at an exceedingly slow pace, all according to the whims of the army. Then, it seems as if fate wanted him to live two lives in the short time he had remaining.

Just after they bought the Gettysburg Farm, he was sent by President Truman to take over the NATO forces in Europe. In 1952 he accepted the Republican Party's nomination for President and served two terms. And while the Eisenhowers continued to maintain their beloved home in Gettysburg, their efforts at using it for anything more than a weekend home away from the White House were continually frustrated.

Eisenhower as President would bring dignitaries, after their serious meetings at Camp David, to the relaxed atmosphere of the Gettysburg Farm. It seemed in keeping with the man. In the serious business of war, his fine touch for the human element and that incredible grin, as broad as the Kansas plains from whence he came, had melted and forged an alloy as divergent—and as strong—as all mankind for the common purpose of casting off a German tyrant's chains. In the postwar world, he achieved much the same thing once the "official" serious business was over and he could get the great leaders of the world in amongst his prize-winning black angus cattle and watching where they stepped, or out on the battlefield of Gettysburg where he could explain the horrid, heart-breaking results of the failure of diplomacy.

But, it always seemed, during the decade of the fifties, the Eisenhowers could never spend quite enough time on the farm.

Finally, in 1961, after his Presidency was over, he and Mamie retired to the farm where Confederate soldiers had once wandered. Ike worked during the day in an office in what is now the Admissions Office of Gettysburg College, writing his memoirs and meeting with politicos and business associates. Sadly, after fifty years serving his country, Dwight Eisenhower only got to spend eight years living in what he and Mamie considered to be their only home. On March 28, 1969, at the age of 78, the general died.

The Eisenhower Home ca. 1955/56
(National Park Service).

Mamie Doud Eisenhower lived another ten years at the farm, and although she enjoyed her privacy, she still donated much of her time and her good name to charitable organizations in the community of Gettysburg and nationwide. For the rest of her life, as some of her friends still living in Gettysburg relate, she worried when things were not quite right at the house, because that was not the way "The General" would have had it.

But the history of the house itself goes back much further than when the Eisenhowers owned it. The General and Mrs. Eisenhower gave the property to the U. S. Government in 1967 with the stipulation that they would be able to maintain a lifetime tenancy in the house. After Mrs. Eisenhower died in

1979, the National Park Service made plans to open the house to the public as the Eisenhower National Historic Site.

When the Eisenhowers first bought the house in 1950 they remodeled. Underneath the 100-year-old bricks that were part of the original Redding family farmhouse, they were astonished to find a 200-year-old log cabin. Unfortunately, it was so deteriorated that it could not be saved, but Mamie, with an eye toward the history of the place, requested that the architects save as much of the older structure as they could and incorporate it into the remodeled structure. The kitchen fireplace and bake oven and some of the brickwork were retained, as well as some of the ancient shutters, floorboards and beams.

The old log farmhouse predated even the establishment of the town of Gettysburg in 1780, and so was, no doubt, the nucleus of a hard-working, probably large family of tillers of the soil. Without even a town nearby, they must have been pretty much self-sufficient and independent.

No one knows whether the Eisenhowers ever experienced any paranormal activity in their farmhouse that might relate back to the original tenants. But since their passing and the opening of the house to visitors, several strange and unexplainable occurrences have happened repeatedly to the government employees who work there.

The events seem to happen near the end of the day, or in the wintertime when visitors are fairly scarce. The house is normally quiet at those times and there are only one or two people there to witness anything out of the ordinary. One interesting thing about these occurrences is that they have been happening to people who are of fairly high intelligence—historians, college graduates, people with their masters degrees—which may make the events even more believable.

There is the case of the slamming doors. In Mrs. Eisenhower's dressing room there is a set of heavy, sliding, mirrored doors. At least two rangers have heard the doors shut with an audible "bang," as if they were forcibly closed. Being sliding doors, they are not affected by the wind.

One ranger was standing with another when she suddenly heard the distinctive sound of the doors slamming shut. The odd part is that the ranger with her heard nothing. Other than their supervisor who was in her office in another part of the house, they knew they were the only ones there. The ranger who hadn't heard the slamming realized something was wrong because of the deathly pale color the other government employee's face had assumed.

They went to their supervisor and told her the story. Being a rational individual, she told them to go upstairs and close the sliding doors with some force to experiment and see if that was indeed the sound at least one of them heard.

Up they trudged. The doors were opened and the experiment took place. The one ranger didn't even have to ask the other if that was the sound she had heard—her pale, sheet-white face again told the whole story.

Two other rangers were out at the house, once again on a cold, wintry February day in 1984 when there were no visitors at the farm. A fine day to catch up on research, thought one ranger, and proceeded to go into the kitchen, part of the original section of the house. He had been engaged in research for a half-hour or so when he heard distinct footsteps descending leisurely down the inside back stairs. He knew what the sound was like because he had heard literally thousands of visitors take that same stairway on their tours.

He called to his associate, assuming she had been checking the house and had come down to find him. No answer. He called again. Still no answer. He got up, walked up the stairs and all through the house, finally finding his fellow ranger. (In a later conversation he stated that he had felt uneasy and sort of "sensed" that someone else was there.) His partner had been nowhere near the stairs for the last half-hour. Assuming that perhaps another ranger had entered or perhaps the unlikely possibility that a visitor had walked down to the farm, they searched the house, she going one way around it and he the other. They met and confirmed that they were the only two in the house.

Fortunately, by then it was close to the time for them to leave. According to the woman ranger, as they stood there after their thorough search of the house, they both heard distinctly, on the soft carpeted stairs that once felt the footfalls of an American President and his First Lady, again the footsteps of someone slowly descending.

They locked the house up quickly and left.

And there is that frequent whiff of perfume that wafts ethereally down the stairs, around the house and lingers especially near the maid's room. It has been associated with Mrs. Eisenhower's favorite scents. Yet all her perfume bottles sitting by the side of her bed upstairs for display to visitors, remain tightly capped.

It was the anniversary of the great general's death. The female ranger mentioned above was at the back door of the house when she heard someone coughing. It wasn't a normal cough, but the hacking, hard cough one hears from someone of a previous generation, who had smoked from an early age before the deadly consequences of the habit were well known. She turned and walked to where she had heard the hacking—the butler's quarters—to see if she could help whatever poor visitor it was that was suffering so. As she approached the butler's quarters, the fierce coughing ceased. Rounding the corner she saw that there was no one any where near the back of the house.

One maintenance person who was stationed in the house alone after hours continued to hear the soft, crackling rustle of the type of crinolines worn on special formal occasions—such as inaugural balls—in the 1950s. She heard the distinct sound so often and so clearly in the evenings that she began to wear a portable tape player with earphones so she wouldn't be disturbed from her work.

And finally, one day after she had been working alone at the house and had locked up the building as she was leaving, she happened to glance back at the house. The shade covering Mrs. Eisenhower's bedroom window slowly raised, then lowered again, as if to make sure that whomever it was at the farm was indeed leaving the grounds.

The rangers privately propose numerous theories as to whom it might be that still dwells within the confines of the beautiful home. Though painstakingly remodeled and cared for as a retirement sanctuary for one of the greatest men of the century and his wife, the home and their long retirement together was still denied to them by a country that found it needed him far too much to ever let him go.

Endnotes

A Wrinkle In Time

[1] Tucker, Glenn. *High Tide At Gettysburg*, 261.

[2] Haynes, Martin A. *History of the 2nd New Hampshire Volunteer Infantry in the War of the Rebellion*, 159.

[3] While signing books in Harpers Ferry, West Virginia, a gentleman approached and offered the information that he had been in Gettysburg that year as a reenactor and had seen the rounds of ammunition just after my friend had received them and had returned to camp. He swore to their absolute authenticity saying they looked as if they were fine museum pieces.

Slaying Days In Eden

[1] Elwood Christ, research on the Sheads' House located in files at the Gettysburg Borough Office.

[2] I remember being interviewed by some of his students in the past as a source for their student papers, and finding many of the stories I collected in their papers. Hopefully, in return for my cooperation with their papers, they won't mind my relating some of their research.

[3] When paranormal occurrences continue to happen at one venue and are observed by many different people at different times, the venue is said to be "haunted."

[4] Data collected for the unpublished papers of Raymond Carpenter, Jan. 25,1980 paper; Kurt W. Hettler, Jan. 24,1980 paper; Jose V. Pimienta, Jan. 27,1983 paper.

Twice Hallowed Ground

[1] Veil, Charles H. "An Old Boy's Personal Recollections and Reminiscences of the Civil War."

A Cavalryman's Revenge

[1] Thomason, John W. *Jeb Stuart*.

[2] From an unpublished letter from Mrs. Hitner to Mrs. Hastings, July 6, 1863, located in the Military History Archives, Carlisle Barracks.

[3] Mrs. Ralph Mitchell, noted Stuart scholar was friends with Mary Marrow Stuart (Mrs. Drewry Smith) the granddaughter of Jeb Stuart, stated that according to the family, Stuart did visit Carlisle in 1859 on his six months leave of absence from the army in the west.

Lower Than Angels

[1] See *Ghosts of Gettysburg*, "The Tireless Surgeons of Old Dorm."

Castaway Souls

[1] The biographical information of Jennie Wade was carefully collected from numerous sources and compiled into an excellent historical work entitled The Jennie Wade Story, by Cindy L. Small and published by Thomas Publications.

Off-Off Broadway

[1] Elwood Christ, Gettysburg Historian, has done a remarkable job researching the houses in town for the Gettysburg Borough. His work resides in the Borough Office.

[2] Dr. Charles Glatfelter, an unpublished script for a slide program on early Adams County, located at the Adams County Historical Society.

Townsmen of a Stiller Town

[1] Quote is a paraphrase from A.E. Housman's "To an Athlete Dying Young."

[2] See *Ghosts of Gettysburg*, "Black Sunset," p. 59.

[3] See *Ghosts of Gettysburg*, "The Inn at Cashtown," p. 72.

[4] This author rode for the National Park Service for four years during that time period. Never, to my knowledge, during the entire time we had the horses, were they ever taken out after dark.

Fall of the Sparrow

[1] Hill, Douglas and Pat Williams. *The Supernatural*, p. 85.

[2] Hill, Douglas and Pat Williams. *The Supernatural*, p. 84.

Death's Feast

[1] *Ghosts of Gettysburg*, p. 26.

[2] See *Ghosts of Gettysburg*, p. 22 for the details of the battle action in the area, and of the subsequent burial, exhumation of the bodies, and stories of other hauntings in the vicinity.

[3] Jose V. Pimienta. "An Investigation into the Folklore and Apparitions of the Gettysburg College Area," unpublished paper done in January 1983 for Dr. Charles Emmons's course in Sociology. Dr. Emmons kindly opened his files to me. It is interesting to read the papers for which I was used as one of the sources for ghost stories I heard of the battlefield in the late 70s and early 80s.

Pirouettes in Quicksand

[1] See *Ghosts of Gettysburg*, "The Devil's Den," p. 19.

[2] The quote comes from an article by A.W. Tucker, "Orange Blossoms," *National Tribune*, January 21, 1886, and is cited in an excellent and comprehensive article "Our Principal Loss Was In This Place," by Kathleen

Georg Harrison, in Gettysburg: *Historical Articles of Lasting Interest.* (Morningside House, Inc. Dayton: July, 1989.) The Orange Blossoms was the rather unusual nickname for the 124th New York Regiment.

3 The quote is from *New York at Gettysburg*, vol. 2, pp. 869-870, once again collected for her article "Our Principal Loss..." by Kathleen Georg Harrison.

4 From an unpublished letter entitled "The Last 24 Hours of General John F. Reynolds," by Charles H. Veil, April 7,1864.

Acknowledgements

Meeting and speaking with people has always been the most interesting part of this job of writing. Though writing has been described as a solitary profession, and it is true that much of it is done in solitude, the occasional contact with others is not only enjoyable, but vital to the production of any book. People have helped me in innumerable ways; from the obvious, of relating their paranormal experiences on the battlefield, to the subtle, of lending encouragement when they saw I needed it. To each and every one, I say thanks.

But I must say an especially heartfelt "thank you" to the following people who helped with this book in very special ways: Roscoe Barnes, III; Beth Bestrom; Elwood Christ; Gregory A. Coco; Jim Cooke & Davey Crockett; Sue U. Currens; Dr. Charles Emmons and the researchers and writers of term papers including Jose Pimienta, Kurt Hettler, Raymond L. Carpenter, Charles M. Shively; Dorothea Fasig and her son Mike; D. Scott Hartwig; David T. Hedrick of Special Collections, Gettysburg College, Musselman Library; Mary J. Hinish; Ray Hock; Corporal Michael Hofe; Karyol Kirkpatrick; Elaine McManness; Stephanie Lower McSherry; Georgette Myers; Manuel Otero of the American Print Shoppe in Gettysburg; Winona Peterson; Greg Platzer; Dr. Walter Powell; Robert Prosperi; Colonel Jacob M. Sheads; Don and Bev Stivers; Danette Taylor; Jeane Thomas; Marsha Taylor-Tyree; Bob & Jane Wright.

To those with whom I spoke who are not included in these acknowledgments, my sincerest apologies. Notes get lost or misplaced very easily in the mental and physical whirlwind my life becomes when writing a book.

And to all those of you who called and wrote to relate your own paranormal experiences on the battlefield, thanks. If your story is not included in this volume it doesn't mean I didn't believe you. Time and space constraints are very real to a writer and must be strictly adhered to. Besides, as the supernatural experiences continue to occur out on this great battlefield, you may someday find your own story included in *Ghosts of Gettysburg III*!

O Death, old captain, it is time! Set Sail!
This land palls on us, Death! Let's put to sea!
If sky and ocean are black as coal,
You know our hearts are full of brilliancy!

*   *   *

Pour forth your poison, our deliverance!
This fire consumes our minds, let's bid adieu,
Plumb Hell or Heaven, what's the difference?
Plumb the Unknown, to find out something new/

—Charles Baudelaire

About The Author

Mark Nesbitt was a National Park Service Ranger/Historian for five years at Gettysburg. During his tenure with the National Park Service, he had the opportunity to spent time in nearly every historic house on the Park. Living in Gettysburg since 1971 has given him a unique "insider" perspective from which to write his popular *Ghosts of Gettysburg* series.

Mark's stories have been seen on *The History Channel, A&E, The Discovery Channel, The Travel Channel, Unsolved Mysteries*, numerous regional television shows, and heard on *Coast to Coast AM*, and regional radio. In 1994, he created the commercially successful *Ghosts of Gettysburg Candlelight Walking Tours*® based on the stories from his books.

Other books in print and/or ebooks by Mark Nesbitt:
Ghosts of Gettysburg
Ghosts of Gettysburg III
Ghosts of Gettysburg IV
Ghosts of Gettysburg V
Ghosts of Gettysburg VI
Ghosts of Gettysburg VII

A Ghost Hunters Field Guide: Gettysburg & Beyond
Fredericksburg & Chancellorsville: A Ghost Hunters Field Guide
Civil War Ghost Trails
Cursed in Pennsylvania
Cursed in Virginia
Haunted Pennsylvania
The Big Book of Pennsylvania Ghost Stories
Blood & Ghosts: Haunted Crime Scene Investigations

*Haunted Crime Scenes: Paranormal Evidence From
     Crimes & Criminals Across The USA*

If The South Won Gettysburg
*35 Days to Gettysburg: The Campaign Diaries of Two
     American Enemies (Reprinted as The Gettysburg
     Diaries: War Journals of Two American
     Adversaries)*
*Rebel Rivers: A Guide to Civil War Sites on the
     Potomac, Rappahannock, York, and James*
*Saber and Scapegoat: J.E.B. Stuart and the Gettysburg
     Controversy*
*Through Blood and Fire: The Selected Civil War
     Papers of Major General Joshua Chamberlain*

Connect with **Mark Nesbitt** on Social Media:
     facebook.com/mark.v.nesbitt
     twitter.com/hauntgburg
     markvnesbitt.wordpress.com
     foursquare.com/hauntgburg
     goodreads.com/author/show/19835.Mark_Nesbitt